The Early Internet

Collected Articles

Tamar Frankel

Professor of Law, Emerita

Boston University School of Law

Fathom Publishing Company

Anchorage, Alaska

ISBN 978-1-888215-88-5

Library of Congress No. 2023919568

Printed in the United States

TamarFrankel.com
Fathom Publishing Company
PO Box 200448, Anchorage, AK 99520-0448
fathompublishing.com

TABLE OF CONTENTS

INTRODUCTION

This booklet describes Tamar Frankel's involvement in the beginning and early Internet development principally between 1998 through 2001. The materials appeared previously in law reviews and other journals, on ICANN websites and in other locations.

We thank the publications that generously granted permission for their materials to be included here. Their materials enrich the booklet with various or developing points of view.

CELEBRATING AN IMPORTANT WOMAN IN ICANN'S HISTORY[1]

Sally Newell Cohen

7 March 2022

SVP, Global Communications and Language Services, ICANN

Ahead of International Women's Day tomorrow, ICANN is celebrating an inspiring woman who played a key role in the formation of ICANN and the creation of the multi-stakeholder model.

Born in Tel Aviv in 1925, Tamar Frankel studied law and began her career as an attorney for the Israeli Air Force. She went on to become an Assistant Attorney General for Israel's Ministry of Justice.[2]

*Tamar Frankel,
Professor Emerita
Boston University School of Law.*

After moving to the United States, she studied at Harvard Law School. Now a Professor Emerita, she has taught at Boston University School of Law since 1968. Professor Frankel teaches and writes about financial regulation, fiduciary law, and corporate law.

(All footnotes have been added.)

1   Reprinted with permission. © 2022 ICANN, Internet Corporation for Assigned Names and Numbers, https://www.icann.org/zh/blogs/details/celebrating-an-important-woman-in-icanns-history-07-03-2022-en (last visited Dec. 23, 2023).

2   Tamar Frankel's childhood and early years in Israel, including her time in the Haganah, are detailed in her memoir LIVING IN DIFFERENT CULTURES (2019).

Professor Frankel also played a key role in establishing ICANN. In 1998, the U.S. Department of Commerce issued a White Paper that proposed transferring the management of the Internet to a nongovernmental entity. In response, a host of businesses, governments, and technical experts from around the world formed the International Forum on the White Paper (IFWP) to devise a plan that satisfied the government's requirements.

Because such an entity was unprecedented, and because of her expertise in corporate governance, Professor Frankel was asked to help design a not-for-profit corporation.[3] She chaired IFWP meetings in Reston, Virginia; Geneva; and Singapore, and helped the stakeholders come to an agreement on how the corporation should function.[4]

As a result of these negotiations, ICANN was born. Professor Frankel remained involved in the organization during its early

---

3   The IFWP was described as follows in bulletins inviting stakeholders to attend one or more of four international meetings in July and August 1998:

> The IFWP is an ad hoc coalition of professional, trade and educational associations representing a diversity of Internet stakeholder groups, including ISPs, content developers, trademark holders, networkers, intergovernmental groups, policy experts, end-users and others. This coalition has come together to sponsor a framework of coordinated international meetings, to be held around the world, at which stakeholders will discuss the transition to private sector management of the technical administration of Internet names and numbers as outlined in the policy "White Paper" recently released by the United States Government. These international meetings are open to all Internet stakeholders, who are encouraged to support this on-going process. https://web.archive.org/web/19981206105122/http://www.ifwp.org/ (last visited Aug. 15, 2023).

Substantial information on early ICANN activities appears in the Hearings before the Subcommittee on Science, Technology, and Space of the Senate Committee on Commerce, Science, and Transportation (June 12, 2002), *available at* https://www. govinfo.gov/content/pkg/CHRG-107shrg92929/html/CHRG-107shrg92929.htm (last visited Aug. 15, 2023).

4   Internet Stakeholder Associations to Advance White Paper Process, *available at* http://web.archive.org/web/19990420010952/http://www.ifwp. org/press.html (last visited Aug. 15, 2023) (the first regional IFWP meeting at the Hyatt Regency, Reston, Virginia, is chaired by Professor Tamar Frankel Emerita—a world-renowned expert on incorporation—of the Boston University School of Law—the two-day event will seek to identify key issues, views and opinions on the areas left open by the White Paper to private sector development).

days, including testifying about ICANN before the U.S. House Committee on Science, Space, and Technology.[5]

According to Professor Frankel, the creation of ICANN shows that if people look beyond their individual interests and work together toward a shared goal, they can build something that is greater than what they could have achieved alone. "When you begin to fight, you can lose everything," she said. "When you cooperate, you don't gain everything, but you are assured of something."[6]

To learn more about the history of ICANN and the contributions of instrumental people like Professor Frankel, visit the ICANN History Project.[7] An interview with Professor Frankel will be featured in an upcoming video on the ICANN History Project's webpage.

---

5   House Report No. 105-847, 105th Cong., 2d Sess., Summary of Activities of the Committee on Science, Hearing Volume No. 105-78 (Oct. 7, 1998).

6   Numerous examples in Tamar Frankel's life reflect her recognition of the benefits of cooperation enjoyed by those who do truly cooperate in achieving a desired goal. Many of these appear in her memoir, LIVING IN DIFFERENT CULTURES (2019), and in McDevitt, *Conviction, Moral Fortitude Define Lifetime Achievement Winner Tamar Frankel*, COMPLIANCE WEEK (May 16, 2022).

7   *See* https://www.icann.org/history (last visited Aug. 15, 2023).

Excerpts of Tamar Frankel's Remarks

The following passages are excerpts taken from meetings or emails to the ICANN board of directors or to ICANN committees in which Tamar Frankel advised the Board or Committee on a matter of interest relating to the subject matter being considered. When necessary, bracketed information is provided to give the context.

Applicable Law

Just two comments: First, the applicable law is not the law governing individual members of the board (persons or corporations) but the law governing the institution—ICANN.

Second, the law applicable to a contract among institutions is usually the law in which the contract is made. The internal affairs of the parties can be governed by different laws and yet the relationship between them can be governed by the law governing the contract. In addition, contract parties may determine the laws that govern their relationship. For example, an SO organized in France can contract with ICANN and (they can) agree that the relationship will be governed by NY law.

Simple! Happy new year. Tamar (January 14, 1999)

Governance and Structure

Governance can be viewed as an efficient mechanism for problem solving. If spam is a problem for so many parties that a combined effort avoids duplication and makes the solution less expensive, then a "governance" or "self-governance" mechanism is likely to arise. Whether it will be world-wide depends on whether the problem is wide spread. Whether ICANN will be the mechanism should depend on whether it is the least expensive and most suitable body, AND whether we prefer one entity to do the job or many entities. This choice may depend on whether the preference for efficiency is greater than the preference of avoiding concentration of power.

One last point: The Internet is like a market because there is no control over membership or use. These are guided by the invisible hand. But markets must have a structure, such as standardization. The Internet also must have a structure. The structure requires some governance-central authority to establish the rules of the game. The important decision is where to draw the line, and avoid standards that are not necessary for the creation of successful markets. Same issue is true of ICANN.

Tamar (April 13, 1999)

Global Open Meetings

To those who brought so many people from all over the world to the meeting in Berlin. Many, many thanks and compliments. You are breaking new grounds to permit global open meetings.

Tamar (May 27, 1999)

Selection of ICANN Board Members

I was the one who did not believe in the (then proposed) selection process of ICANN's board and who spoke, whenever I could, for membership and election. But I also recognize that ICANN has to be built. The current board is composed of people whom I respect. It has the support of the government, conditioned on changes.

I think that criticism of ICANN is absolutely essential until such time as it will be structured correctly . . . . The fear, mistrust and disrespect among the various group interests in this area is blatant and clear. Each of the groups must gain legitimacy in the eyes of the other. I believe and hope that the US government will not relinquish control over ICANN until it is satisfied that its current deficiencies will be eliminated or reduced. If the executive does not do so, the Congress or other government agencies will.

Tamar (November 24, 1999)

Development of ICANN

I am more patient. I think that you and others are doing a good job of pressing for the right structure that would command trust and legitimacy. It is not that I am uncritical. It is that so long as I see movement, I will not make a final judgment. Further, I do not believe that ICANN is a sham. Sham means that what you see is not there. I do not believe that ICANN is a sham. It is not acting the way you (and sometimes I) want it to act. That is different from sham. . . .

In the U.S., legitimacy is gained more by the trustworthiness of the system than that of the leadership. We trust the banks

5

but not necessarily the bankers. We trust the constitution and political system but not necessarily the politicians. This balance may be different in other countries. So, from the U.S. perspective, the ability of the system to ensure good successors is crucial. I believe that in ICANN's case, the ability of the leaders to establish such a system is the main test.

Tamar (January 14, 2000)

A View of Cooperative Competition*

In the early 1990s, a former student asked me to design and run the establishment of a not-for-profit organization in Virginia. Sure; I agreed.

Only later did I learn about the unique nature of this not-for-profit corporation. This corporation was designed to hold the key to the Internet that had been developed by the United States Army. The management of the Internet was later transferred to a highly-respected expert—Jon Postel.[1] As the Internet was expanding and became more promising, international business organizations claimed the right to participate not only in its use, but also in its control.

The "techies" and the business parties argued before Congress and lobbied the White House, but no agreement was reached. The White House recommended that the parties meet in another attempt to come to an agreement. They planned a meeting in Virginia for the not-for-profit organization that I was to design. Needless to say, I knew nothing about the Internet, but I did know something about corporate law, which I was teaching.

Before the meeting, the experts tutored me about the Internet and the organization as it existed. A stunning number of e-mails poured in, some of which demanded fifteen minutes for their position. This demand, it was explained, reflected the practice of previous public meetings when each party was allocated fifteen minutes to make its presentation.

It became clear that the past procedures and practices would not bear fruit. Instead, when I came to the hotel in Virginia, I asked for a number of changes. First, no newspaper reporters were

---

* Excerpt from Frankel, LIVING IN DIFFERENT CULTURES, pages 23-24. *See generally* Oral History of Tamar Frankel, Fifth Interview 1-18 (Mar. 22, 2008), *available at* https://www.americanbar.org/content/dam/aba/directories/women_trailblazers/frankel_interview_5.pdf (last visited Aug. 15, 2023).

1 *See* Jon Postel, Posthumous Recipient, https://internethalloffame.org/inductees/jon-postel (last visited Aug. 15, 2023).

to be allowed into the meeting. Second, the hall in which the members of all parties were to meet would be divided into five spaces and each space would have a blackboard.

The meeting participants numbered about 500 persons. Instead of fifteen minutes, the process would follow different rules: The five blackboard stations each held part of the design of the corporation that the participants were about to create. Participants were encouraged to move from station to station and argue to their hearts' content. However, by 6 p.m. that day, each group must report on any agreement reached concerning the items noted in the stations: (i) the name of the organization, (ii) the number of the directors, (iii) the position of International Countries and (iv) a few other such items. They should report only what they agreed upon. And they should determine who would report the results.

At 6 p.m., each group came forward and its representative proudly presented its decision, the name, the structure and other details were generally but clearly established. There was a feeling of "high" in the audience, a feeling of achievement, achievement of something great and productive. It was a "winning" but a different kind of winning.

Thereafter, I traveled to Switzerland and Singapore and spoke to a group in South America. The interested parties adopted the structure, and the Internet Corporation for Assigned Names and Numbers (ICANN) was born. That was the time to withdraw and regain my life.

However, the lesson was surprisingly clear. When people have the opportunity to build together something great, new, and ambitious, they may find far more satisfaction in this activity than in winning against each other to retain the status quo or winning a position at the expense of, and against, others, or destroying the existing structure or gaining the exclusive power for their own benefit. That "something new" became the Internet. The arguments continue, as business takes a far more active part, as do various world States. Legal, business and political problems abound. But the Internet exists.

This happened years ago. The United States has currently relinquished to the world most, if not all, of its power over ICANN. My story focuses on one point only: Competitors, especially if their expertise complements each other, may find that working together is better for both: not arguing and rejecting but instead agreeing. The agreement may be more rewarding than standing rigidly on a position.

Governing by Negotiation: The Internet Naming System

Governing by Negotiation: The Internet Naming System*

Tamar Frankel

I. Introduction

This Article is about the governance of the Internet naming system. The subject is fascinating, not simply because the naming system is an important system affecting the Internet, although it is; and not because the Internet is important, although it is. The subject is fascinating because it offers a rare opportunity to examine and learn from the evolution of an incoherent governance structure. The naming system is special in that it is the product of a new technology; it reflects the changes and pressures brought by the new technology, and involves the interests of government and private entities, domestic and international. And while this combination is complex and special, the players are known and their motivations are quite familiar: a quest for power and money, a professional pride and national patriotism, and deep commitments to various ideologies. Can we predict or even speculate with some certainty how this governance system will develop? Regardless of whether we can, what lessons can we learn from what we see? How should we approach the questions? How can we generalize our findings?

The governance of the naming system involves the actors in the system's infrastructure—the registries, registrars, governments, the Internet Service Providers, and the Internet Corporation for Assigned Names and Numbers ("ICANN"). The naming system is

---

* Tamar Frankel, *Governing by Negotiation: The Internet Naming System*, 12 Cardozo J. Int'l & Comp. L. (2004), *available at* https://scholarship.law.bu.edu/faculty_scholarship/913 (last visited Dec. 23, 2023). Reprinted with permission from Cardozo Journal of International and Comparative Law.

designed as a pyramid, with the one source root at the top.[1] This pyramid is operated by a number of entities.

The naming system presents many questions. Does ICANN's policy-making power matter; and if so, to whom? I do not deal with these issues, but I address them briefly because they constitute part of the context of my inquiry. ICANN's policy-making is an important matter. It coordinates some activities among the actors in the naming system infrastructure. It offers, mostly through others, some services for the actors in the infrastructure. It has authority to create new Top Level Domain Names in the United States under ".us," or otherwise. It has authority to create new country code Top Level Domain Names ("ccTLDs"), and to approve (or disapprove) the "delegation" of the operating power of top-level domain names, including ccTLDs. It is involved in, and can affect, matters concerning conflicts between trademark holders and domain name holders. It is involved in determining whether a particular entity is an organization entitled to use ".org," or an educational institution entitled to use ".edu." ICANN may have the power to determine the use of domain names in languages other than English. And the list can be extended to the qualifications and the duties of registrars and registries that manage top-level domain names at different levels.[2]

ICANN's powers involve money. Every power that ICANN may exercise and every request that must be directed to it, can, and usually does, carry a price tag. ICANN can set charges for whatever services, permissions, consents, or requests for consents it entertains. To the extent that ICANN can define the scope of its powers and the price tags that it attaches to the exercise of its powers, it may indeed build a significant empire that involves the infrastructure of the Internet naming system and affects the operations of the Internet.

1   Under this root, in a secondary line, are ccTLDs, such as ".uk" or ".au," and under them in the hierarchy are Top Level Domain names, such as ".com," ".org," ".gov" and ".edu." Under these Top Level domain names, such as ".edu," are names of educational organizations, such as Boston University, and under the names of the organizations could be additional layers, such as ".law," and at the bottom of the pyramid are the names of individuals, such as "Tamar Frankel."

2   See KIM G. VON ARX & GREGORY R. HAGEN, *Sovereign Domains, A Declaration of Independence of ccTLDs from Foreign Control*, 9 RICH. J.L. & TECH. 4 (2002) (providing a short, coherent description).

To What Extent Does ICANN's Empire Concern the Users?

Indirectly, ICANN affects users in two ways. First, individuals may be affected by the amounts they have to pay to the registrars. To the extent that ICANN is instrumental in encouraging competition among the registrars and registries, it can influence the price of domain names. Moreover, to the extent that ICANN has power over the transfer of domain names from one registry or registrar to another, it can induce competition among them, and consequently, impact the users. In addition, ICANN's decisions and the processes it imposes to protect trademark holders can greatly affect small businesses. In particular, if the protection offered by ICANN's regime encompasses pejorative use of names by trademark holders, there may be a detrimental impact on small businesses which were tardy in registering names. In their defense, entrenched trademark holders will likely assert that such businesses conceded the use of particular names by failing to register.

How Serious Will These Issues Be in the Future? How Important Will the Naming System Become?

To the extent that search engines, such as Google, relieve users from resorting to domain names in searching for specific sites, the pressure on short and easily remembered domain names may be eased. Furthermore, work is being done on a new system of naming that may be more suitable for the current and future states of the Internet, especially if it can be combined with telephone and fax numbers for a comprehensive digital information source.

Yet, some of the issues discussed above cannot be resolved by a "telephone book" type of search, such as Google. There are pressures to support the continuation of the system. For instance, the ccTLDs are being considered as alternatives to geographical addresses for other communication systems. If this development takes place, the importance of ccTLDs will grow, and they are likely to carry with them the current naming system. Moreover, the longer the system remains in place, the harder it might be to change it, for people are creatures of habit and the current system acquires important stakeholders that may not easily give up their benefits. Thus, the current system is unlikely to disappear soon.

The focus of this article is not on ICANN or its ambitions or on any problems of accountability that it may pose.[3] Neither is the focus on the technical solutions to the existing system. This article focuses on an incoherent governance system (including, but not limited to, ICANN), and its future development.

A. *The Governance of the Naming System: Tracing the Power Structure*

The governance of the naming system consists of a few loosely connected powerful entities. ICANN is a pivotal component because it has some management powers over the system, and because the naming system is designed as a natural monopoly. However, although ICANN has indicated a clear desire for more power and money, it is not necessarily the strongest member of the group as its powers are vested by default.[4] Its competitors, mostly foreign governments and United Nations institutions, such as the International Telecommunication Union ("ITU"), can offer the same or even better services than ICANN. These competitors refrain from doing so by "negative consensus"— none of the participants agree that any of the others will control the Internet naming and numbering system. Indeed, if the ICANN agenda threatened any of its competitors' vital interests, these competitors would signal that they are ready to take over, or consider taking over, ICANN's functions. While ICANN and its representatives may yearn for more leverage with respect to

---

3   *See* Tamar Frankel, *Accountability and Oversight of the Internet Corporation for Assigned Names and Numbers (ICCAN), Report to the Markle Foundation* (2002), *at* https://papers.ssrn.com/sol3/papers.cfm?abstract_id=333342 (last visited Dec. 23, 2023).

4   *See* Tamar Frankel, *The Managing Lawmaker in Cyberspace: A Power Model*, 27 BROOK. J. INT'L L. 859 (2002) (examining the puzzle of ICANN as a weak monopoly. Although it controls the Internet naming system and its "root," ICANN is quite weak in its freedom to exercise this power and has a limited ability to raise funds. The article analogizes ICANN's environment to that of a monopolist in a "contestable market" where the monopolist achieves its position because it can profitably offer a price which is lower than the price that other competitors can offer. However, if the competitors are able to enter and exit the market without cost or with very low cost, their ability to do so constrains the monopolist from raising its prices. If the monopolist charges higher prices, its competitors will enter the market, and when competition drives the prices down to an extent that makes it unprofitable for them, the competitors will exit. Hence, in order to enjoy its preferred position, the monopolist will choose not to raise its prices above the prices that its competitors find profitable).

governance of the system, its potential competitors effectively limit its ambitions.

Accordingly, ICANN is a weak member of the naming system governance structure, except for three facts. First, ICANN derives its power from a contract with the United States Department of Commerce. The United States is not inclined to relinquish its influence on the system any time soon. Second, the actual operation of the root is in the hands of another organization in contract with both the United States Department of Commerce and ICANN. Third, ICANN's competitors have not managed to establish a sufficiently stable coalition for a sturdier power structure.

The strongest support for ICANN, however, is the fear of Internet disintegration. That is what feeds cooperation among all the parties.

This glue of cooperation is reminiscent of the first constitutional assembly in the United States. The various States had different objectives and many disagreements. What brought them together was the War of Independence against the British. Together they were stronger. Defection meant a danger to survival of each and all. In the Internet, defection from some, but not all, structural arrangements may mean a danger to connectivity, for each and all, which is also a form of survival. The naming system may belong to this structural arrangement.

However, parties' motivations in changing the status quo differ. ICANN, for example, is interested in signing contracts with, and gaining funding from, the registries of the ccTLDs. Most registrants are far less eager. As one of ICANN's directors noted, "no agreements can be reached unless all parties want to play."[5]

None of the other parties involved has a significant power advantage over the others. Even though the Department of Commerce seems to be in control, it is also bound by legal limitations in exercising power over ICANN. The purpose of this self-limitation becomes clear when one examines the history of ICANN's creation. During the late 1990s, when the Internet emerged as an "information highway" and a tool for commercial expansion, the United States government was hard pressed by a number of governments to relinquish its control over the root

---

5   *ICANN Intrigues—The Jonathan Cohen Interview—Part 2,* DEMYS NEWS SERVICE, *formerly at* http://www.demys.net/news/2002/10/02_oct_22_icann_intrigues.htm (Oct. 22, 2002).

and "internationalize" the naming system. The United States, however, was not of the same mind, and some strongly argued for the United States retaining its power, especially since American taxpayers had financed the building and development of the Internet in the first place.

The United States government reacted by offering a binding self-limitation that significantly weakened its control over the root. The United States government limited its own ability to change its position, under the current federal law. The U.S. facilitated (but did not "establish") the creation of a type of corporation that the government could not directly "control." Under federal law, the executive branch may "establish" and "control" a private sector corporation only pursuant to a congressional statute.[6] Arguably, ICANN is not a government corporation; the executive branch did not establish it, nor does it control it.

Nevertheless, ICANN is strongly bound to the United States. It is a nonprofit corporation organized and governed under California state law, although a very strange type of nonprofit corporation indeed; it still exercises vague and semi-governmental powers. It is subject to the jurisdiction of the United States courts and the California Attorney General. In addition, although the Executive cannot control ICANN as a government corporation, the Executive may, under American law, contract with private sector corporations for the performance of services. The Department of Commerce has entered into such a contract with ICANN and with the actual operator of the root (Verisign). The Executive has discretion to change the operator and manager of the root by contract.[7] Because the contracting party is the Department of Commerce, Congress has a measure of power to supervise the Department, and its activities, including the contractual arrangements that it has made with ICANN. Congress can also require the General Accounting Office to research and investigate such contract arrangements, and the Office has indeed done so

---

6   *See* Government Corporation Control Act of 1945, 31 U.S.C. §9102.

7   Memorandum of Understanding Between the U.S. Department of Commerce and Internet Corporation for Assigned Names and Numbers, *at* https://www.ntia.doc.gov/ntiahome/domainname/icann-memorandum.htm (last visited Aug. 15, 2023) (original agreement); National Telecommunications and Information Administration, U.S. Department of Commerce, Management of Internet Names and Addresses, *at* https://www.ntia.doc.gov/ntiahome/domainname/icann.htm (last visited Aug. 15, 2023) (listing subsequent amendments).

upon request from Congress.[8] Nonetheless, the U.S. government in fact has the ultimate power over the root. ICANN is "potentially in a position to say no (to requests by other countries) but the United States has its thumb fully on the group and if the United States says someone doesn't get on, then they don't get on."[9]

Initially, the U.S. government expressed an intention to relinquish its ties with ICANN after the first three-year contract with ICANN had expired. However, when the time arrived, the U.S. government instead renewed the contract and shortened the contract period to one year. In September 2003, the government again renewed the contract, this time for three years.[10] Today the United States has shown no inclination to fully relinquish its control of the root, as tenuous as that control may be. One can speculate about the reasons for this change in policy. Among them may be the fact that ICANN was expected to develop as a stand-alone semi-international government entity accountable to the actors in the infrastructure of the Internet, its servicers and its users. It was expected to develop legitimacy and stability as a governing body. That, however, did not happen. Perhaps as the importance of the naming system has risen, the possible disadvantages of relinquishing control over the system have risen as well. For these reasons, it seems that the United States would like to maintain the status quo, but reduce the tensions that have arisen as a result of its control.

An examination of the naming system's history and the history of other relationships among actors in the Internet infrastructure seems to reflect loose organizations, splinters, and further splinters. It is as if the organizations reflect the Internet's structure. This hybrid of organizations and loose relationships is not used in the business context. ICANN, however, is not a

---

8   *See* 31 U.S.C. §712 (granting Comptroller General power to investigate use of public money); 31 U.S.C. §717 (granting Comptroller General power to evaluate programs and activities of United States government); 31 U.S.C. §716(a) (requiring agencies to make information available to Comptroller General and granting Comptroller General power to inspect agency records). The Comptroller General has the power to delegate its duties to the General Accounting Office. 31 U.S.C. §711(2).

9   *ICANN Intrigues—The Jonathan Cohen Interview—Part 2, supra* note 5.

10   Memorandum of Understanding Between the U.S. Department of Commerce and the Internet Corporation for Assigned Names and Numbers, Amendment 6, *at* https://www.icann.org/general/amend6-jpamou-17sep03.htm (Sept. 17, 2003) (last visited Aug. 15, 2023).

business organization. It is led by business interests but exercises functions that are part governing and part technical "policies," with which businesses are not familiar.

The multi-faceted nature of the issues is also extraordinary. For example, ccTLDs raise issues on various levels. One issue concerns the "ownership" of the names. This issue may relate to the trademark area and to the right of third parties to use the name. Another view of the names relates to the right to insert the names in the root. Only that appearance would allow Internet messages to reach their destinations. A third aspect of the names is the right to manage them, and that issue involves the right of the registries to appear in the root. Without such a right, the registries will not receive Internet messages for transfer.

In the last analysis, however, the existence of a country and the business of the registries of the ccTLDs depend on their appearance in the root. The party that has the power to decide which name will be inserted and which will be removed masters much power. It need not necessarily be the party that operates the root.[11] It is the one that makes the decision. However, even this power is not unlimited. It depends on the consensus of the other Internet infrastructure actors to look to the root as the authoritative address book. It also depends on the absence of any alternative system that can bypass the root and reach the same results. Although there may be some routes through others who are on the root, these roundabout ways are not preferred. Not everyone agrees with this statement. Some suggest the creation of a different root. Arguably, the registries of the ccTLDs can create their own coordinating entity and refrain from resorting to ICANN or the operator of the current main root. But this system does not seem to have attracted the registries.

B. The Nature of the System's Power Structure

To the extent that foreign governments wish to make changes in the root or in the identity of the registries that manage their ccTLDs, the governments must resort to ICANN. ICANN's decisions are likely to be influenced by the Department of Commerce's position, which may be influenced by Congress. All actors have constrained powers. Some constraints are self-imposed, like those

---

11 This party need not have the authority to determine the trademark aspects of the names or even other aspects of the system, such as qualifications of the registries and registrars.

of the United States Department of Commerce. The government of France commenced an antitrust action against ICANN, but decided to put the action in abeyance, at least for the time being. There is also a self-imposed limitation, but with greater discretion. The powers of all parties, however, are constrained by the potential powers of the other parties. This is not necessarily, however, a balance of power situation like the one found in most Western constitutions. The limitations that each party exercises on the powers of others are negotiable and not institutional. This distinction will be discussed later in more detail.

In sum, ICANN's power hangs on the thin reed of a short-term contract with the Department of Commerce. But the power is strongly supported by the desire of the U.S. government to maintain its hold on this thin reed. The other power holders, although unhappy with U.S. dominance, are reluctant to cede control to any other power holder, and none are ready to terminate their connectivity with the Internet. Even China, a country that has a strong political drive to control the substance of the communications of its citizens through the Internet, maintains its existing channels to the Internet.[12]

The governance of the naming system is unique in its vagueness both with respect to the exercise of power and the substance of the policies that regulate the exercise of the power. This type of structure can best be described by the ad hoc limits that each party can impose on the others rather than by the areas reserved to each party by consensus, or by the functions that each party performs, or by rules which the majority of the stakeholders support.

The governance of the Internet naming system is at a crossroads, as it has been since its creation. An analogy to two familiar governance models shows that it fits neither. One model is a power structure prescribed by a general law and equally applicable to all members of defined classes of the governed as well as the governing bodies. The law can be changed only in accordance with a prescribed process that involves not only the lawmakers but also others to whom they are accountable. Although the system is operated in part by ICANN, which seems

---

12 *China Steps Up Internet Control with Video Surveillance in* CHANNEL NEWS ASIA, *formerly at* http://www.channelnewsasia.com/stories/afp_asiapacific/ view/81320/1/.html (Apr. 22, 2004) (last visited Dec. 23, 2023) (stating that although China is trying to reap the benefits of the Internet, it also attempts to control the content of the messages that reach China).

to be organized under a state corporate statute, the governance of the naming system as a whole does not fit this model. In addition, ICANN's organizational structure is evolving. The identity of the stakeholders is still subject to debate and continuous study. The ability of the recognized stakeholders to nominate governing bodies is not secure. In fact, the idea that ICANN should reflect a democracy, and especially that the democracy should include the users, has all but been abandoned as unworkable. There is too great a danger of capture by unacceptable elements and too great a danger of unacceptable nominees to the board and other governing bodies.

The latest attempt to find a way to democracy without these dangers is the establishment of delegates to nominating committees and the establishment of the board's own Governance Committee.[13] All these activities are legal in the sense that they are backed by ICANN's articles of association. The substance, however, commands further experimentation and study. That approach should be commended as truly cautious. Realistically, rather than a matter of utopia, however, the studies tend to lengthen and maintain the status quo.

As a matter of utopia, I would like to see some principles, standards, guidelines, and specified mechanisms to achieve them. These would have the effect of limiting discretion and a test by which to judge discretionary decisions. Since these are missing, I am basing my observations on reality as I see it. In addition, ICANN's articles have become increasingly flexible. Most of its constitutional provisions are in the bylaws and not in the articles of association. Not that it makes much difference in this case, since there are few other bodies that can voice their concerns and enforce their opinions on any changes. Bylaws, however, are determined by the board. Even though they are intended for limited purpose, such as process and organizational matters, these bylaws contain significant constitutional powers. The changes are therefore made whenever the board finds them desirable or wise, but with little input. To be sure, the board holds meetings on the changes at times and can then make the changes it likes. This reality renders the bylaws and ICANN's structure very flexible.

---

13 *See* Preliminary Report, *at* https://www.icann.org/minutes/prelim-report-12mar03.htm (Mar. 12, 2003) (last visited Aug. 15, 2023) (nominating committees from academic organizations and ccTLDs and establishing a Board Governance Committee).

ICANN reacts not within its structure and rules but by changing its structure and rules.

The other model, which the governance of the naming system resembles superficially, is the market. The parties use their power to strategically negotiate a division and balance of power, and the financing of governance activities. Parties may establish power relationships by private agreements and understandings. Usually such agreements affect only the parties, but there are cases in which they influence third parties.

Parties that agree with ICANN may divide and balance power relationships pursuant to contracts, which may contain "constitutional provisions" that seemingly affect only the parties—ICANN on the one hand and the other party on the other hand. These contracts, however, include a provision that requires parties to a contract with ICANN to comply with ICANN's future policies.[14] The sample agreement available on the Internet provides that specifications and policies in an appendix apply at the commencement of the agreement and that new or revised ICANN specifications and policies applicable to the Sponsoring Organization shall be established according to procedures that comply with ICANN's bylaws and articles of incorporation and with procedures that provide the sponsoring organization input into the decision-making process.[14.1] ICANN's policies will therefore be deemed the law of the naming system land, just as congressional laws apply to all without a condition of supporting consensus. The problem is that ICANN is not constituted like the Congress, and is subject to far fewer accountability measures than either a private sector or a public sector corporation. Moreover, ICANN's powers are only vaguely defined and are subject to heated debates. Therefore, its freedom to design future policies would open the door to expansion of its powers. These policies can vest in ICANN's broad discretion not only with respect to the contract party but also with respect to its own powers vis-a-vis the

---

14   Model ccTLD Sponsorship Agreement, §5, *formerly at* http://www.icann. org/cctlds/modeltscsa-31jan02.htm, *now see* Model CCTLD Sponsorship Agreement Triangular Situation, *available at* https://www.icann.org/en/ system/files/files/pw-icann-sa-20jun03-en.pdf (last visited Dec. 24, 2023).

14.1 Model CCTLD Sponsorship Agreement Triangular Situation, Paragraph 5, *available at* https://www.icann.org/en/system/files/files/pw-icann-sa-20jun03-en.pdf (last visited Dec. 24, 2023).

contract party. The provision "gives ICANN a stranglehold over different [countries'] domains."[15]

It is not surprising that foreign countries and the registries of ccTLDs objected to the contract language. The more parties sign the contract, however, the more expanded ICANN's power can become. This pattern will seemingly continue, unless the contracting parties agree, at some future date, to enter the naming arena as competitors and restrain ICANN by taking it over, or by breaching their contracts and seeking its invalidation.

Thus, the current governance of the naming system seems to reflect the second model of a market more than the government of a private or public organization. To be sure, markets also function under a number of basic rules to which all players must subscribe. But these rules can be negotiated with greater freedom and flexibility. In the case of ICANN, the flexibility is even greater. The rules are established not between two parties to a bargain but between a ruler (monopolist) and the ruled (all the parties that interact with the monopolist). History seems to repeat itself. James I, the British King, granted "odious monopolies" that led to a public outcry and culminated in the Statute of Monopolies of 1624.[16] Most importantly, the rules may end up affecting ICANN's power not only vis-a-vis the contracting parties but other third parties as well.

If the contract provisions are the same for all parties, the contracts form an unintended coalition among those who signed them. If the contracts differ, depending on the power relationship among the parties, the contracts can be analogized to "private laws." The market in which ICANN and other power holders operate is a market for rules.

Usually, rulers do not negotiate individual governance deals with their subjects, but seek to establish rules to which a majority of their subjects agree or reach consensus. But in the case of "private laws" some parties may fare better than others depending on their bargaining powers and depending on the support they receive from others. Thus, the rules are not predictable and leave broad discretion to the ruler. The contract format gives the false impression of a consensual "democratic" regime rather than a

15 Kieren McCarthy, *Kangaroo Domain Court,* THE REGISTER (London), Dec. 13, 2001, *formerly at* http://www.theregister.co.uk/2001/12/13/kangaroo_domain_Court/.

16 *See* Donald S. Chisum et al., PRINCIPLES OF PATENT LAW 13-14 (2d ed. 2001).

regime of rules imposed from above. In fact, the contract format is likely to open the door to corruption, as the history of corporate law and other laws demonstrates.

Legislatures granted corporate charters not on the basis of a general statute, but on the basis of private laws and legislator corruption.[17] Scandals of corruption led to the general corporation laws that we have today. The government has no discretion to deny applicants a charter, except as defined in the law. Otherwise it must grant a charter. Further, the rules under which the charters are granted apply equally to all applicants. This does not mean that ICANN's method leads to similar corruption. It means that it could lead to such a problem and emulate history.

All participants in the governance structure of the naming system follow two principles, with which all seem to agree. First, all participants hold their power in trust for the well being of the Internet and its users worldwide. Second, country code registries are holding their power in trust for the citizens of the country whose name they service. But these general principles are not sufficient to create acceptable detailed rules by which all parties will use their power to achieve the common goal, or induce them to trust each other to implement the goal in the same way. Hence, the existence of the "private ordering" mechanism. There is, however, one rule or strong preference that constrains all players, and that is the preference to maintain, and be connected to, the Internet. This preference drives all players to cooperate.

C. A Proposed Approach: Game Theory

How will ICANN's governance structure develop, and what form will it ultimately take? Assuming that no party is strong enough to dictate the answer to this question, how can the answer be predicted? In this Article, I propose a method that may lead to a way of thinking about it, rather than a plain prediction. I focus on the interaction among the main actors of the naming system and I attempt to discern patterns of behavior. If these patterns continue, then through them, a "habit" or "path dependence," as well as a consensus, may emerge, leading to rules that will form a more stable and predictable governance structure. This result, however, may merely constitute a hope. We may find that the

17   Lewis D. Solomon et al., CORPORATIONS: LAW AND POLICIES: MATERIALS AND PROBLEMS 5 (1982) (describing how legislative privilege of charter resulted in temptations and corruption). As incorporation became a "matter of economic necessity," it led to the passage of general corporate laws.

parties' behavior is so strategic as to make future behavior and binding rules unpredictable.

For the purpose of this discussion, I assume that the structure of the Internet naming system remains the same, and that ICANN and its potential competitors will continue to "muddle through" under few rules to which all subscribe. Although it seems as though muddling through is entirely fortuitous, opportunistic, political, subjective, changing, and undisciplined, I believe that there are pointers towards more consistent trends.

That is where game theory can help. One type of game theory is a zero-sum game. In such a game, one party's gain is another party's loss. The calculation of such a game is relatively simple. But reality is usually more complex, and to reflect this complexity, there developed a non-zero-sum game theory. Under that theory, in most cases, both parties will either gain or lose unless they cooperate. More often, the pie must be sliced and shared or there will be no pie. This situation resembles that of the parties involved in the Internet naming system.

Game theorists use mathematical models to quantify results and control wayward ideas and assumptions. This paper does not use a mathematical model, and I do not have the knowledge to develop such a model. But the ideas outlined in this paper can be tested by a mathematical model and implemented with the use of available data. I do not purport to offer solutions to the various conflicts that arise between governments, the registries of their country code names and others, but the suggested method is helpful to provide a structure for a discussion on the current and unknown future issues.

I started by attempting to limit the subject to the interaction between governments and the registries of the countries' top-level domain names ("ccTLDs"). The relationship among these two parties is particularly interesting, not only because the relationship has not yet been settled, but also because the governments constitute the ultimate power holders in the market of the naming and numbering system. I quickly discovered, however, that this focus can only be a starting point. Like most interactions concerning the naming and numbering system, the interactions between the governments and the ccTLD registries involve ICANN, the United States, other governments, and other actors in the market for power over the Internet naming system. The relationships cannot be limited to these two parties without considering the others' potential and actual intervention. Those other power holders form the context and the environment in which the governments and the registries operate and relate.

In sum, the naming system today has not matured into a governance structure under predictable fixed rules. The main rules, especially in relation to the governments and their registries, are in a state of flux and at a stage of negotiation between ICANN on the one hand, and the governments and registries on the other hand. It may well be, however, that if the non-zero-sum game that the parties are currently playing could be modeled, the model would uncover latent patterns of governance to which all parties subscribe. This paper is a call to start this research process.

D. A Thumbnail Sketch of a Non-Zero-Sum Game Theory

Game theory is used to study conflict situations involving opposing party interests.[18] In such situations, each player selects a strategy, or an action or set of actions, and the payoffs, or results to the parties, can be quantified and arranged on a matrix.[19] A game is considered a "zero-sum game" if one party's loss is another party's gain, and the sum of all payoffs to all players, positive and negative, is zero.[20] An example of such a zero-sum game is a two-player poker game in which one player's winnings equal the other player's losses.[21]

A game can also be a "non-zero-sum game," which is fundamentally different from a zero-sum game. In a non-zero-sum game, it is possible for all players to gain or for all of them to lose.[22] In such a game, "there is no universally accepted solution . . . no single optimal strategy that is preferable to all others, nor is there a predictable outcome."[23] The players have both complementary and non-complementary interests. Therefore, their game includes elements of cooperation as well as competition. This game is more

---

18   *See* J.D. Williams, THE COMPLEAT STRATEGIST 2-3 (rev. ed. 1966).

19   *Id.* at 14-20.

20   *Id.* at 15.

21   *Id.* at 14-15.

22   *See id.* at 15.

23   Janet Chen et al., *Game Theory, formerly at* http://cse.stanford.edu/classes/sophomore-college/projects-98/game-theory/ (last visited Aug. 24, 2004), *now see* https://cs.stanford.edu/people/eroberts/courses/soco/projects/1998-99/game-theory/index.html (last visited Oct. 30, 2023).

likely to reflect the reality that an optimal solution is neither automatic nor easily found.

One example, often used in literature, of a non-zero-sum game is the "battle of the sexes." Both a husband and wife have a very strong preference to spend the evening together, but she wishes to go to the boxing match while he wants to go to a ballet performance. Since both strongly desire to go together, if each has his or her way both lose more than they gain.[24] However, this leaves them in a quandary, in which a solution is neither automatic nor uniform.

A number of strategies are available to this couple, depending in part on their own preferences.[25] First, each party can change its own utility values, as well as that of the partner, by adding events. For example, if the wife buys two tickets to the boxing match, the couple would lose the value of the tickets if they go to the ballet event. The husband may value the loss of the ticket prices more than the discomfort of watching the boxing match.

Second, the couple may decide to forego both events altogether and to choose an event that is acceptable (but not as acceptable as the original choice) to both, such as the theater. To be more effective in seeking this solution each party may develop a "min-max" strategy. Each party can determine how far it will go either in its demands or in giving in to the demands of the other. Each party may make its strategy known to the other party. Consequently, each party may find a second-best choice that would be sufficiently satisfactory to both parties.

Third, the parties can use threats and promises to induce the other to agree. A "threat" in a non-zero-sum game is a statement communicated to another player that the player would select a certain strategy, hoping to influence the behavior of the other player.[26] For example, in a buyer-seller situation, the seller could state that it would not sell the item for less than a certain price. The seller is hoping to encourage the buyer to agree to buy at the

---

24   See Morton D. Davis, GAME THEORY 88 (rev. ed. 1983), now see Morton D. Davis, GAME THEORY: A NONTECHNICAL INTRODUCTION (2003). See also Andrew M. Colman, GAME THEORY AND ITS APPLICATIONS: IN THE SOCIAL AND BIOLOGICAL SCIENCES (2d ed. 1999).

25   One strategy, which is inapplicable in our case, is when one or both parties refrain from communicating. If they do not communicate, they can neither threaten nor promise rewards to each other in the future.

26   See Morton D. Davis, GAME THEORY 101 (rev. ed. 1983), now see Morton D. Davis, GAME THEORY: A NONTECHNICAL INTRODUCTION (2003).

seller's desired price, knowing that if the sale is not made, the result will be adverse to both players.[27] Similarly, in the "battle of the sexes" situation, either player may threaten to attend his or her preferred event alone, if necessary, in an effort to influence the spouse to attend that event as well.[28]

"A threat is effective only to the extent that it is plausible."[29] A threat is less plausible if the possible payoff to the threatening party is more adverse.[30] If the players cannot communicate, then neither can they threaten.[31] Since a threat requires communication, a player that refuses to communicate with the other not only eliminates the possibility of a threat from the other player, but eliminates his own threat as well. Other threats and promises are possible as well. The husband may threaten to not accompany his wife to her favorite events in the future in light of the high utility that he has put on the current event. The parties may also use rewards. For example, the wife may agree to give the husband the book he liked or the trip he was hoping for. Exchanges may be arranged as well, such as "we alternate in going to events each party likes."

Fourth, a party dealing with numerous other parties may adopt the strategy of "divide and conquer," attempting to negotiate with each of the other parties separately. Even though the lone negotiator may reduce her costs when negotiating with a group rather than with an individual, she may confront a stronger opposing party and have less of an opportunity to gain from a disparity in bargaining power.

Fifth, the parties may agree to have their conflicts resolved with the help of a third party, such as a good friend or a psychiatrist, if in a family conflict, or an arbitrator or mediator if in a business conflict.

The example of the battle of the sexes represents everyday familiar relationships. But the example is surprisingly suitable to relationships in other contexts as well, including relationships within commercial and political organizations, and among market parties. I use the term "market" very broadly to denote

---

27 *Id.*

28 *Id.*

29 *Id.*

30 *Id.*

31 *Id.* at 95.

non-organizational relationships, even though markets are also subject to rules and required patterns of behavior without which no interaction among parties can exist for very long.[32]

The actors in the Internet naming system infrastructure play a "simultaneous game." A 'simultaneous game" is one in which all players make decisions, or select a strategy, without precisely knowing the other players' strategies. Even though the decisions may be made at different points in time, the game is simultaneous because each player has no information about the decisions of others. Thus, it is as if the decisions are being made simultaneously.[33]

A Nash equilibrium, named after mathematician John Nash, is a set of strategies, one for each player, such that no player has an incentive to unilaterally change its action. Players are in equilibrium if a change in strategies by any one of them would lead that player to earn less than if it remained with its current strategy. For games in which players randomize (i.e. use mixed strategies), the expected or average payoff must be at least as large as that obtainable by any other strategy.[34]

A Nash bargaining scheme may be helpful in the ccTLDs scenario as well. This scheme suggests that the objective of a bargaining party is to make an agreement that is as favorable to it as possible and at the same time avoid demands that would put obstacles on making an agreement. A party that is willing to settle for terms that are only slightly more advantageous to it than not having an agreement is likely to make an agreement. A party that insists on favorable terms is less likely to make an agreement. However, if one party knows the "break point" of the other, it would insist on that break point to its advantage. That is why parties act as if they are uninterested in agreements when they are desperate to reach one. This is also why parties refrain

32 *See* Tamar Frankel, *The Legal Infrastructure of Markets: The Role of Contract and Property Law*, 73 B.U.L. Rev. 389 (1993).

33 Game Theory Dictionary, *formerly at* http://www.gametheory.net/Dictionary/SimultaneousGame.html (last visited Aug. 24, 2004), *now see* https://www.gametheory.net/dictionary/ (last visited Oct. 30, 2023). Simultaneous games are represented by the normal form and solved using the concept of a Nash equilibrium.

34 Game Theory Dictionary, *formerly at* http://www.gametheory.net/Dictionary/NashEquilibrium.html (last visited Aug. 24, 2004), *now see* https://www.gametheory.net/dictionary/NashEquilibrium.html (last visited Oct. 30, 2023).

from naming their price or demand more than they are willing to accept when they do not know the price that the other party may be willing to accept.

This Article traces the activities of the registries of the ccTLDs, the governments and ICANN, to examine whether they reached equilibrium in their relationship, where they failed to reach such equilibrium, and the direction that they are taking after such failure.

E. The Parties' Utility Function

A "utility function" quantifies the players' preferences so that the payoffs will reflect the change in utility to the parties.[35] In a non-zero-sum game, the parties may have different preferences, and their choice of strategies may depend on their utility functions. In the battle of the sexes example, the husband may love ballet passionately and consider it the most important event of the year, or he might hate the boxing spectacle because of some childhood memory. Each player may have the same or a different intense feeling of altruistic satisfaction in "sacrificing" his or her wishes to the desires of others, or of "winning" and controlling the other, and these feelings may determine strategies. Each party may expect or know that the other will reciprocate (or not reciprocate) in the future in the same or other ways, which may also determine strategies.

Similarly, governments may put different values on Internet connectivity for their residents. For example, China values the commercial benefits of the connectivity, but puts a higher value on controlling the substance of the messages that its residents send abroad, even though this control slows the pace of the messages and reduces the efficiency of the Internet for China's residents. Further, the balance of power and dependence of the parties on each other may not be equal, in which case they may choose different strategies in negotiating with each other.

Not all strategies help reach a long-term solution that is satisfactory to both parties, or even to a single party. Reciprocity can be negative as well as positive. Long-term memories of a party's resentment may backfire in a later situation when the "winner" is more vulnerable. It is not unusual for parties to reach an impasse and either go to their chosen event alone or not go to any event altogether, creating a lose-lose situation. These patterns

35   *See* Morton D. Davis, GAME THEORY 62-65 (rev. ed. 1983).

of behavior can be modeled[36] to provide lessons for those who seek to learn how to behave in the future. The patterns may also help predict the future for those who are locked into their behavior and unlikely to change it.

F. Governance by Contract Negotiations and the Actors' Positions

Had the naming system been governed more by fixed rules and less by negotiations, game theory would not have been very helpful. The theory is useful because the naming system is currently governed mainly by negotiations. We will therefore discuss the negotiations that take place between governments, their registries, and ICANN. In each case, we will identify the weight each party puts on particular demands (the utility function), and the strategies the parties use to satisfy these demands.

As discussed earlier, the power infrastructure of the Internet naming system is composed mainly of governments, registries (and registrars), ICANN, the Internet Service Providers, and the technical community. ICANN's president outlined the "essential participants" in the system as Internet infrastructure providers, major users, the "relevant technical community," and national governments. If market pressures are deemed powerful, then large and small users of the Internet should be included in the list. It seems that governments hold significant power. But the United States government, through its Department of Commerce and the United States Congress, may hold even greater power, although it is exercised somewhat indirectly and discreetly. The root exists physically in Virginia and is operated by a private corporation, Verisign, under a contract with the Department of Commerce.[36.1] The Department has also contracted with ICANN to operate the naming and numbering system, although the scope of ICANN's operational and policy powers are unclear.

---

36   Elmer G. Wiens, *Operations Research-Game Theory, formerly at* http://www. egwald.com/operationsresearch/cooperative.php (last visited Aug. 24, 2004).
36.1 *See generally* https://en.wikipedia.org/wiki/List_of_ISO_3166_country_ codes; https://verisign.com and https://www.ntia.gov/page/verisign-cooperative-agreement (both last visited Oct. 30, 2023).

G. The Governments and ccTLD Registries

1. Applying the Game to the Government-ccTLD Registry Relationship

The relationship between the governments and their ccTLD registries is unique and varied. Like all other participants in this non-zero-sum game, a termination of the relationships between governments and ccTLDs will produce the worst result for both. Governments may not be able to remove registries and appoint others without ICANN's approval. To do so would be to risk possible termination of the connectivity of their country to the Internet. The registries of the ccTLDs will lose their business or their ability to impose their ideology on how the Internet naming system should be managed in their countries, or sustain losses for other reasons. I, therefore, conclude that, for different reasons, the worst scenario for both parties is the termination of the relationship and the endangering of their connectivity to the Internet.

2. The Governments' Utility Function in Relation to the Country Code Name

Most governments are likely to give their country's name a very high subjective value. They may view themselves as trustees of the name for their people. The country's name may represent to its people the identity of the country, its history and the legitimacy of its government. The full riches of patriotism may be compressed and packaged in the country's name. Giving the name, or control of the name, away may result in negative popular sentiment. A country's name can give a purported government the political legitimacy that it may otherwise lack or that may be hotly debated and fought over (e.g., Palestine).[37] Removing the

---

37   To avoid making a political decision, IANA followed a list by ISO 3166 Maintenance Agency, and agreed to the re-delegation of Palestine when Palestine was accorded the status of "Occupied Palestine Territory." IANA, IANA Report on Request for Delegation of the .ps Top Level Domain (2000), *formerly at* http://www.iana.org/reports/ps-report (containing IANA's report and analysis which led to the recommendation to approve the redelegation). *See also* International Organization for Standardization, English Country Names and Code Elements, *formerly at* http://www.iso.org/iso/en/prods-services/iso3166ma/02iso-3166-code-lists/list-enl.html (last visited Sept. 27, 2004), *now see* https://www.iana.org/reports/2000/ps-report-22mar00.html (Mar. 22, 2000), and ISO 3166 https://en.wikipedia.org/wiki/List_of_ISO_3166_country_codes (both last visited Oct. 30, 2023, *now see* https://

name of a splinter opposition party, especially if it uses violence to make its objections known, can silence that party and strengthen the political position of the government. For example, the Spanish government sought the ban of a web site used by Basque militants. The site was registered by an Australian company, with the server in California, and administered in France.

In very few situations, a small country may view its name as a source of income and license it to commercial enterprises (e.g., the television industry). Some ccTLD names are valuable because they happen to form an expression, which would be desirable for companies to have as suffixes in their domain names. The smallest nation on earth, Tuvalu, has earned over $20 million by licensing its ".tv" domain name to media enterprises.[38] Other countries have received desirable ccTLD names and some have sold such names.[39]

In such a case, the government will identify with the business interests of the registries. Such a government's utility function is demonstrated by the following case, which was the first case to involve a ccTLD. In 2000, Expedia, Inc., a U.S. travel service, brought before the World Intellectual Property Organization ("WIPO") a complaint on trademark violation against Domain Network that registered the domain name "expedia.nu." ".nu" is a ccTLD of an island state of 2000 citizens managed by New Zealand. More than 60,000 ".nu" domain names have been registered in Niue, by .NU Domain Ltd., a Massachusetts-based

---

www.iana.org/reports/2000/ps-report-22mar00.html (Mar. 22, 2000), last visited Oct. 30, 2023 (stating the complete list of country names and ISO 3166-1 Alpha-2 code elements—the ISO country code used on the Internet).

38   Charles J. Hanley, *Internet Suffix Nets Cash, Concern for Pacific Nation,* Commercial Appeal (Memphis, Tenn.), July 11, 2004, *at* A15.

39   *See Domains.biz, .info Go Live,* Industry Standard.com, June 27, 2001, LEXIS, News Library, AllNews File (noting that one registrar "offers simulated (top level domains) by using ccTLD names"); *NU Path Offered on Internet,* Australian, Nov. 25, 1997, *at* 22 (noting that Niue, a little-known island nation, is selling its ".nu" ccTLD name; ".nu" is pronounced the same as English word "new" and "nu" means "now" in some languages; because the country is little-known, "its (ccTLD) name carries little national identity outside its borders"); Nick Clayton, *Tonga—The Most Desirable Address?,* Scotsman, July 16, 1997, *at* 2 (noting desirability of Tonga ccTLD ".to"); Joey G. Alarilla, *Infotech Use of Philippines' 'PH' Domain Name Draws Arguments,* Philippine Daily Inquirer, Mar. 12, 2001, *at* 17 (noting concerns about Philippines ccTLD administratm marketing ".ph" name to telephone companies; noting other desirable names including ".mu" (Maurius) ("music"); ".cc" (Cocos and Keeling Island) ("credit card"); ".md" (Moldova) ("health care")).

firm that administered the domain on behalf of the Internet Users SocietyNiue. The registry adopted ICANN's Uniform Domain Name Dispute Resolution Policy for all ".nu" registrations. .NU Domain says it has customers in dozens of countries throughout the world using its services to register ".nu" domain names, among them Coca-Cola and International Data Group. WIPO was ready to apply to the dispute the same principles it applied to disputes concerning Top Level Domain Names.[40]

It is worth noting that governments' utility functions with respect to country code names have been on the rise. This trend is evidenced by the activities of a government committee that advises, and greatly influences, but does not control, ICANN—the Government Advisory Committee ("GAC"). The membership of the GAC is one of the constituencies that could demand control of the root but does not, as long as the other members do not demand control.

In February 2000, this group recommended that the ownership of ccTLDs be explicitly given to the countries that they represent. The GAC's Principles for the Delegation and Administration of Country Code Top Level Domains, states that the managers of ccTLDs, known as delegees, must recognize that "ultimate public policy authority over the relevant ccTLD rests with the relevant government or public authority."[41]

This recommendation constituted a response to situations in which ccTLDs were managed by registries that acted independently of the governments whose names they managed.

> For example, the .pn domain, which was designated for the Pitcairn Islands, until recently was run by a Channel Islands company, one of whose contacts for registration purposes was an island resident. Within a few months of the initial delegation in 1997, though, the island territorial government, along with the United Kingdom,

---

40 Daniel Pruzin, *WIPO Receives First Request to Rule in Country Code Domain Name Dispute*, INT'L BUS. & FIN. DAILY (BNA), Mar. 29, 2000, LEXIS, BNA Library, BNABUS File, See generally WIPO Guide to the Uniform Domain Name Dispute Resolution Policy (UDRP), *at* https://www.wipo.int/amc/en/domains/ guide/ (last visited Oct. 30, 2023). *See generally* WIPO Guide to the Uniform Domain Name Dispute Resolution Policy (UDRP), *at* https://www.wipo.int/ amc/en/domains/guide/ (last visited Oct. 30, 2023).

41 Government Advisory Committee, *ICANN, Principles for the Delegation and Administration of Country Code Top Level Domains*, §4.4 (Feb. 23, 2000), *formerly at* http://www.icann.org/Committees/gac/gac/cctldprinciples-23feb00.htm.

had opposed that delegation, claiming that the domain was being used predominantly for registration of domain names to entities not affiliated with the territory, in exchange for a fee collected by the company.[42]

The GAC did not necessarily require full control by the political governments, but proposed rules for the establishment and delegation of ccTLD non-government registries of the ccTLDs. Thus, the utility function of government can run broadly, from political to social to financial considerations. As the registries become more financially profitable, the allocation of this exclusive business can be used for political and business purposes alike.

ICANN responded enthusiastically to the GAC's recommendations.

> [T]he board of the Internet Corporation for Assigned Names and Numbers signaled its desire to resolve the issue of how much control governments will have over those who operate their country code top level domains, like .uk, sometime this spring. . . .
>
> . . . ICANN also decided to give its staff authority to work with the managers of the ccTLDs, the Government Advisory Committee, and any other interested parties to develop a final proposal on how much control governments have over the ccTLDs. . . .
>
> The GAC issued a recent report that asked for governments to be given control over who could manage a ccTLD. However, the GAC report did not specifically address the thorny question of what the relationship between ICANN and the ccTLD managers would be.[43]

While the issue remains largely unresolved, and dealt with on a case-by-case basis, almost every country has now asserted some form of control over its domain name. Indeed, a recent study by the ITU found, to its surprise, that 43% of countries had ultimate control, with another 30% having taken steps toward gaining

---

42 Jennifer L. Alvey, *Government Group Advising ICANN Wants Nations to Control Country Code Domains,* Electronic Com. & L. Rep. (BNA), Mar. 8, 2000, *at* 232, 233.

43 Jennifer L. Alvey, *Internet May Have New .com-Type Domains Soon if Net Authority Acts on Schedule,* Electronic Com. & L. Rep. (BNA), Mar. 15, 2000, *at* 253.

that control. Only 7% of the countries had no formal control and no plans to change that.[44]

The demands of the GAC, and the actions of its members to take more control, reflect its utility functions. The Committee recommended a number of strong protective measures. For example:

> [N]o private intellectual or other property rights should inhere in the ccTLD itself, nor accrue to the delegee . . . . The delegee should work cooperatively with the relevant government or public authority of the country or territory for which the ccTLD has been established, within the framework and public policy objectives of such relevant government or public authority . . . . The delegee, and the delegee's administrative contact, should be resident or incorporated in the territory and/ or jurisdiction of the relevant government or public authority. Where the delegee . . . [is] not resident or incorporated in the territory and/or jurisdiction of the relevant government, it should nonetheless operate in a way that is consistent with the laws and public policy of that relevant government or public authority.[45]

The GAC recommendations also called on ICANN to "act with the utmost promptness to reassign the delegation" of a ccTLD once a government tenders evidence that the current delegee does

---

44 Michael Geist, *Governments and Country-Code Top Level Domains: A Global Survey* (Feb. 2004), *formerly at* http://www.itu.int/ITU-T/worksem/cctld/ kualalumpur0704/ contributions/ccTLD-KL-003.pdf.

45 Government Advisory Committee, *ICANN, Principles for the Delegation and Administration of Country Code Top Level Domains*, §§4.2-4.6 (Feb. 23, 2000), *formerly at* http://www.icann.org/Committees/gac/gac/cctldprinciples-23feb00.htm, *now see* https://gac.icann.org/principles-and-guidelines/public/ principles-cctlds.pdf, and *at* https://studylib.net/doc/13239776/governments-and-country-code-top-level-domains--a-global-survey. *See also* Internet Domain Name System Structure and Delegation (ccTLD Administration and Delegation), *at* https://nsrc.org/workshops/2004/ccTLD-bkk/info/icp-1. htm (public comment forum), *now see* Governmental Advisory Committee, Principles and Guidelines for the Delegation and Administration of Country Code Top Level Domains *at* https://gac.icann.org/principles-and-guidelines/ public/principles-cctlds.pdf, and Michael Geist, Goverments and Country-Code Top Level Domains: A Global Survey *at* https://studylib.net/doc/13239776/ governments-and-country-code-top-level-domains--a-global-survey (all last visited Oct. 30, 2023). *See also* Internet Domain Name System Structure and Delegation (ccTLD Administration and Delegation), *at* https://nsrc.org/ workshops/2004/ccTLD-bkk/info/icp-1.htm (public comment forum).

not have the support of the relevant government.[46] Also, ICANN should expect cooperation from the government of the relevant country if ICANN determines that the delegate is operating the ccTLD in a way that "threatens the stability" of the Internet or the domain name system.[47]

This last proposal recognizes the dual obligation, established by the founder of the naming system, Dr. Jon Postel, of the registries both to the country whose name they manage and to the Internet in general to whose infrastructure they belong. Presumably, if a registry opposes the government's policy, for example, of using the Internet for developing a country's commerce, the government would have the power to remove the control of the registry.[48] If, in contrast, the government appoints an incompetent registry, the registry may object to the appointment, and ICANN may press to remove the registry.[49]

Not all governments, however, have the same utility function in relation to their names. It may well be that the United States government will part ways with other Western countries. Thus, the Department of Commerce has been considering the possibility of opening the ".us" ccTLD space to the private sector. Compared

---

46   [Reserved]

47   [Reserved]

48   But if the government is oppressive, and the registry is outside the geographical boundaries of the country, a registry may object to transferring its functions for political reasons. Dr. Postel imposed a trust on the registry not for the benefit of the government but for the benefit of the people in the country. Who is to determine whether the government, recognized by other governments and the United Nations, is the representative and true trustee of the people? Under the proposed directives the government and its policies will trump the registry's political views. The policies, however, have not been adopted.

49   Jennifer L. Alvey, *Government Group Advising ICANN Wants Nations to Control Country Code Domains,* ELECTRONIC COM. & L. REP. (BNA), Mar. 8, 2000, *at* 232-33.

> The report also calls on all ccTLDs to have in place a dispute resolution policy. Such a policy should have several principles reflected in it, such as "due regard" for internationally recognized intellectual property law and consumer protection. Alternative dispute resolution procedures should be conducted online, if possible, according to GAC, but should not preclude resort to courts.

The GAC's recommendations *were formerly at* http://www.icann.org/gac/gac-cctldprinciples-23feb00.htm. Background on the ccTLD delegation issue is available on ICANN's website *at* http://www.icann.org/cairo2000/cctld-topic.htm (last visited Aug. 15, 2023).

to England, where the ccTLD is freely used by the private sector (e.g., britishtelecom.co.uk), the ".us" domain name is used almost exclusively by state and local governments. It may well be that the value of ".us" TLD for commercial interests is not as great as in other countries. Commercial interests do not use the ".us" domain, finding it "too cumbersome and complicated." But according to the Department of Commerce, expanded use of the ".us" TLD by the private sector "could alleviate some of the pressure for new generic TLDs and reduce conflicts between American companies and others vying for the same domain name."[50]

Unlike other governments that seem to have a clear position, the United States seems to be ready to consider a broad array of possibilities. In its Request for Comment, the Department of Commerce during the Clinton Administration sought comments on a variety of policy matters relating to the future of the ".us" domain, including: whether ".us" should be treated as an unrestricted top-level domain like ".com;" how second-level domains should be allocated; what role states should play in the allocation and registration of their respective sub-domains; what procedures could be used to minimize trademark disputes within the ".us" domain, and; whether there is a particular kind of entity best suited to manage the ".us" domain.[51]

In addition to the importance of country codes for the respective governments, the names may gain enormous importance in electronic commerce for any country. Country codes have been considered as substitutes for designation of locations, and if that proposal is accepted, they will attain considerable added value.[52]

3. The Utility Functions of the Registries of ccTLDs

In general, a government's value of the name is likely to be higher than the value that ccTLD registries attach to the name, if patriotism comes second to the value of the registries' business. Registries may manage another name and be as successful financially. Some registries, however, view themselves as agents of the state and have the same utility function as the governments, and at least one had a very high utility as a representative of an

---

50 *Commerce Seeks Input on .us Domain; Explores Expanded Private Sector Access,* DAILY REP. FOR EXECUTIVES (BNA), Aug. 5, 1998, *at* A-25.

51 *Id.*

52 Anandashankar Mazumdar, *UNCITRAL Group to Begin Discussions on E-Contracting Treaty at March Meeting,* BANKING REP. (BNA), Jan. 21, 2002, *at* 3.

Internet free of government interference. It should be recognized that the sentiments of the governments with respect to their country's names are likely to be shared by most large governments. This leads to a modicum of a consensus.

H. The Strategies: Assertions of Principles and Threats

How do governments that derive higher utility from their domain names negotiate to support their claims both to the names and to control over the registries of their ccTLDs?

1. To Cooperate or Defect?

As stated, all participants in the power infrastructure of the Internet desire to maintain connectivity and ensure its continued viability. This desire drives the parties to cooperate. If a party does not cooperate, it stands to lose more than the others, since it would lose connectivity to all others while the others would lose connectivity only to one party. The only way in which all parties stand to gain is for all to cooperate fully and to unanimously agree on an alternative. It seems that such a move is far more costly to any of the parties than the status quo.

Another consideration driving the parties toward cooperation is the reduction of risk and uncertainty for the interacting parties. One of the Internet's salient features (and also its strength) is its openness to any change at a higher level. But for some parties, this feature can pose significant uncertainty. It can threaten other values that a party might cherish, such as political stability (as the government defines it). Under these circumstances, a cooperative agreement to reduce the uncertainty may be welcome among parties that share a similar resistance to the uncertainty.

Parties may weigh passive and active cooperation differently, depending on the value they assign. Thus, registries of ccTLDs value active cooperation by contract with ICANN less than ICANN values the cooperation by contract. In addition, the parties weigh the terms of the proposed or negotiated contracts differently. While ICANN is more eager to sign and receive power and funding, the registries are far less eager to actively cooperate.

Lastly, even though all parties would rather interconnect with the Internet via the main root, there are some alternatives to such interaction via other means. These alternative means are not as attractive and are more costly. The choice of such means may also lead to negative pressures by other parties. If registries of ccTLDs choose alternative means, at a higher cost to them, the cost of ICANN, for example, may be even higher. Not only will ICANN lose the opportunity to induce the parties to contract on its terms, but the defecting party may show the way to others, and start a movement towards the alternative.

2. Legitimizing Claims by Principles-Based Actions

Principles do not necessarily help cooperation. Principles, however, can clarify the real parties to the contract. Strong principles can be persuasive, especially to those who are like-minded. Here are a few principles that were used and the users who used them:

a. Name ownership in rem.

This principle conflicts with the asserted rights of others to use a country's name, and indirectly with ICANN's power to designate the names that appear in the root. Governments that place a very high value on the country's name have asserted that the name constitutes property, that this property belongs to them, and that the registries are the government's agents. Thus, the governments have asserted their dominion over their name and registries of the name. They have sued companies that have registered the country names as Internet addresses.[53] South Africa has gone further and enacted legislation that "provided for government control of domain administration, instead of government participation."[54] It asserted its rights to its domain name against the claims of a private business enterprise that had used the name in its business.[55] The GAC recommendations also propose clear ownership principles. These principles, however, have not been adopted by ICANN.

b. Power to appoint the registries.

This principle conflicts with ICANN's asserted power to designate the names that appear in the root, with the asserted rights of registries that were appointed by Jon Postel. The principle

---

53 *ICT and Telecom; Battle for SA Domain Caught in a Legal Web*, Africa News, Jan. 10, 2003, LEXIS, News Library, AllNews File (noting litigation by South Africa and New Zealand governments).

54 *Deadline for .za Domain Board Nominations Extended*, Global News Wire (South Africa), Nov. 21, 2002, LEXIS, News Library, AllNews File.

55 *Virtual Countries, Inc. v. Republic of South Africa*, 148 F. Supp. 2d 256 (S.D.N.Y. 2001) *aff'd*, 300 F.3d 230 (2d Cir. 2002).

also conflicts with ICANN's asserted power to disqualify registries. Additionally, the principle may conflict with the assertion of registries that they were vested with their position by Jon Postel. A number of governments asserted their right to appoint the registries to their ccTLDs. These asserted rights conflict with ICANN's assertion of authority to approve or disapprove the "delegation" of the power to manage their ccTLDs. While governments derive their asserted right from the name, ICANN derives its asserted right from the management power of the root.

In the struggle, governments can exercise their power over their registries so long as the registries are within their physical jurisdiction, and so long as the identity of the registries does not change. In such cases the governments can control the registries by passing laws to this effect. However, when governments wish to change the identity of the registries and substitute one registry for another, ICANN, or rather the U.S., has the upper hand. The laws may be insufficient to formally effect a change without ICANN's consent. Unless a registry is designated in the database of the root, the transfer cannot be completed. ISPs will not recognize the new registry and will continue to recognize the old one. The laws, however, have powerful effects of threats, as discussed below.

Conflicts between a government and its existing registry can arise when the two disagree on the use of the Internet and the power of the government to designate another registry, as illustrated in the Australian example. The government was patient, but was not willing to give up its full priorities. It was a zero-sum game and the registry lost. The government did not choose the direct route of legislation to root out the registry, but rather approached ICANN to mediate and reach an agreement. The Australian government has been historically supportive of ICANN, since the use of ICANN suited its purposes and undermined the legitimacy of the registry that claimed entitlement to the function by the appointment of Jon Postel. Since ICANN is the offspring of Dr. Postel, the registry's claim to legitimacy was undermined by the advantage of the Australian government. I suggest, however, that if ICANN had supported the registry, the Australian government could have passed a law to transfer the registry to its choice.

Underlying the relationship between governments and their ccTLD registries is a conflict of principle. While many, if not most, governments claim the name as their own, some registries (and ICANN) claim their right to manage the ccTLD, on behalf of the free enterprise of the Internet. This claim then leads through ICANN to the United States as the source of their entitlement. Ultimately, arguments of principle pit governments that assert property rights to their names against the United States. Therefore, the main non-zero-sum game is not only between the governments and their registries, but also between these governments and the United States government. In the last analysis, these conflicts led to disagreements between foreign countries and the United States through ICANN, or through the actions of Dr. Jon Postel. Both acted for the United States under contract, although Dr. Postel was controlled more closely by the U.S. than ICANN is.

These principles, however, are interesting in two respects. Their users wish to change the status quo with respect to the powers of the United States. The opposition, wishing to maintain the status quo, resorts to the past regime. Regardless of the merits, the relative power of both sides may guide the answer. The current holder of the power (the root) may have the upper hand for now. The weakness of the principles is noticeable when one party uses the opposite principle in other contexts. Thus, ICANN advocates change when it aims at formalizing relationships especially with the registries of the ccTLDs, while the latter seek refuge in the status quo and the past.

3. The Bargains

When a country seeks ICANN's approval to change its registry, ICANN might use the opportunity to extract benefits for its approval, such as added funds of which it is usually short. The benefits it can extract depend in part on the strength of the applying country. Small countries and their registries have succumbed to ICANN's demands, signed its contracts and are paying up. Australia is a prime example, although that country has long supported ICANN, and therefore may have found the terms of its contract more acceptable. In this context, the balance of power among the parties seems to dictate the outcome.

Agreements between ICANN and ccTLD registries are the products of long negotiations, and may have resulted in compromises. But the balance of the compromises is difficult to assess without further investigation of the processes. Because the negotiations are among few parties, and the contracts could affect third parties that did not take part in the negotiations, some of these contracts have been renegotiated after they were completed in light of the strong objection of the third parties. This process of renegotiation is the result of the one-to-one talks among a few parties when the subject matter of the contract is in fact a rule.

Two main issues have held up agreements between ICANN and ccTLD operators: power and money. Some ccTLDs would like to play "a greater role in ICANN's decision-making process."[56] The few recent agreements between ICANN and the ccTLD registries allowed "new or revised ICANN specifications and policies applicable to the (registry)" to "be established according to procedures that comply with ICANN's bylaws and articles of incorporation," although ccTLDs are allowed input into the development of these policies.[57]

In addition, the ccTLDs "have clashed with ICANN on questions about their financial contributions to ICANN."[58] The agreements require ccTLDs to make financial contributions to ICANN "based on ICANN's total funding requirements . . . developed by ICANN on the basis of consensus."[59] Most registries are unwilling to fund ICANN's expanded operations without a stronger power position in the organization. Meanwhile, the registries of the ccTLDs have attempted to gain more power in ICANN's structure. That step may conflict with governments' assertion of full ownership and control over their country codes. Governments' involvement in ICANN's affairs is also limited in principle. Nonetheless, they are acquiring power increasingly. This renders weaker the registries that assert independence, and pits foreign governments against the United States when their interests conflict.

4. Threats

A law is a powerful signal to ICANN (and indirectly to the Department of Commerce) that another government's demand

---

56   *ICANN Reaches Agreement with Operator of Japan's Country Code Top-Level Domain,* Int'l Bus. & Fin. L. Daily (BNA), Mar. 1, 2002, LEXIS, BNA library, BNABUS File.

57   *See, e.g.,* ICANN, *ccTLD Sponsorship Agreement (.au),* §5, *at* http://www. icann.org/cctlds/au/sponsorship-agmt-25oct01.htm (Oct. 25, 2001) (last visited Aug. 15, 2023) (hereinafter ICANN).

58   Dugie Standeford, *Names Council Cracks Down on Non-Dues-Paying Constituencies,* Wash. Internet Daily, June 6, 2002, LEXIS, News Library, AllNews File.

59   Government Advisory Committee, *ICANN, Principles for the Delegation and Administration of Country Code Top Level Domains,* §4.6 (Feb. 23, 2000), *formerly at* http://www.icann.org/Committees/gac/gac/cctldprinciples-23feb00.htm.

for a change in the registry of a ccTLD is serious. It is a signal that, without weighty reason, such demand should be accepted. The government can contact the U.S. Department of State and, through its own channels, exert pressure on ICANN. The problem of the governments is that their own laws and changes of the registries—"delegees"—cannot have effect without ICANN's approval directly or indirectly by the Department of Commerce or the Congress. This is one of ICANN's powers, which the governments, in their recommendations, desired to eliminate.

In conflicts involving a government or governments, a larger country has more clout than a smaller country, because it can reduce the Internet population by a larger number (thereby preventing other countries from communicating with a large number of users) and yet maintain interconnectivity within the country. Yet, such a country is also more vulnerable if its population and its economy depend on communications with others through the Internet. Therefore, the number of Internet users in a country can be more important in determining a country's negotiation strength than its number of citizens. In addition, a greater impact on world commerce gives a country more power to make demands concerning the Internet. However, the impact of a limited Internet exposes a country to more risk if it needs not only internal interconnectivity but also connection to world commerce.

The impact of a party's threat is closely related to its accompanying conduct. The extent to which it binds itself to a demand signals to the other parties the weight of its utility function. For example, the European Union demanded recognition of its name ".eu," even though the Union is not a recognized country under the United Nations rules. In 2000, ICANN's reaction was negative, citing various problems that recognition of such a regional name would raise.[60] As the demands of the European Union continued, Congress reacted by proposing legislation, which, if passed, would have had the effect of precluding ICANN from recognizing ".eu" before it recognized another Top Level

---

60   Bruce A. McDonald, *International Intellectual Property Rights*, 35 INT'L LAW 465, n.45 (2001), LEXIS, News Library, AllNews File.

domain name (".kids"), which would be used in the United States.[61] However, during the same year, ICANN changed its position and stated the reasons why it might concede to the Union's demand. ICANN found a legitimizing rule that enabled it to accept ".eu" even though it was not on the primary United Nations list.[62]

In April 2002, the European Union's Council of Telecommunications Ministers approved a new ".eu" domain to operate on the same level as ccTLDs. These government actions represent a strategy of a commitment to a position in the nature of a threat. The governments' claim to a name is as strong as their claim to the territory. The European Union that claimed a new ccTLD, however, did not comply with the definition of a country that ICANN has followed because the European Union is not a member of the United Nations. To show its commitment to back its demand, the European Union passed a directive declaring its new Internet name.[63] The actions have effect within the countries' geographical boundaries. But the actions also have effect on their gaming towards other registries and ICANN. The law supports the demand for recognition. This law is difficult to change, not only because of the process involved, but because of the loss of face and political requirement for explaining a retreat from the demand. Thus, a law allows the government to regulate the registry within its boundaries, but the law is also used to notify anyone who might have power to claim influence over the use of the name that the government is committed to asserting its rights

---

61   Kevin Murphy, *European Domain May be Scuppered by US .kids Bill,* COMPUTERWIRE, July 3, 2001, LEXIS, News Library, AllNews File. However, in December 2002 Congress instead passed legislation creating the new second-level domain "kids.us." *See also* Laura Rohde, *Bush Signs Bid for Child-Safe Domain Names,* INFOWORLD DAILY NEWS, Dec. 5, 2002, LEXIS, News Library, AllNews File.

62   While the Internet Assigned Numbers Authority ("JANA") has a policy to create new ccTLDs only for codes on the ISO official list of two-letter country codes, the ISO has another list of codes for administrative subdivisions of these countries ("the ISO 3166-1 list"), and this list includes ".eu." ICANN directed JANA to delegate country codes not on the ISO 3166-1 list as ccTLDs "only where the ISO Maintenance Agency has reserved a slot on its exceptional reservation list that covers "any application of ISO 3166-1 that needs a coded representation in the name of the country, territory, or area involved.'" For criticisms of ICANN's decision, *see* Dugie Standeford, *.EU Decision Stirs Criticism from TLD Applicants,* WASH. INTERNET DAILY, Oct. 16, 2000, LEXIS, News Library, AllNews File.

63   *.eu Gets Go-Ahead: New Domain for Europe to Go Live in 2003,* INTERNET MAG., May 1, 2002, *at* 13, LEXIS, News Library, AllNews File.

to the name, and to the registry of the name. It is a threat to other parties involved, and it sets the price of the other party's attempt to disagree.

The European Union showed its commitment to the name by passing a law. The United States agreed, but made the agreement provisional. We may expect the name to continue so long as the Union wishes, but we might see a longer period for a final recognition of the name to emerge, maybe after some formal request to ICANN or a diluted form of such a request. In addition, we may see some agreement on the part of the European Union to pay ICANN directly or through its registry, and that may be accompanied by a place for the European Union on the advisory committee of the governments.

The concessions may be predicted by an estimate of the value that each party will attach to it and by the irreversible commitment that it will make to its demand. However, so long as their demands are met, it seems that the governments are not as committed to alter the basic current arrangement. They may recognize that the ultimate say on the naming system is with the United States. The United States—both Congress and the administration—may recognize that the naming system is not theirs to control, manipulate, or use as they wish. They also must recognize that the dissatisfaction by other governments, or by some independent ccTLD registries, cannot be ignored and must be addressed.

The reaction of the United States to the demands of other countries to "internationalize" the Internet demonstrates a similar method. The United States bound itself under its own laws to reduce its control over ICANN by denying ICANN's status as a government corporation (established and controlled by the government) and reducing its power over the root by maintaining contractual control.

ICANN's adoption of this strategy is demonstrated in the following story. In the opinion of its staff, ICANN needs funding to perform its job effectively, and the ccTLD registries are a source of funding.[64] As long as they do not sign contracts with ICANN, their undertaking to pay is less assured. ICANN proposed to increase

---

64   Juliana Gruenwald, *ICANN Plan for Restructuring Draws Fire from Various Groups,* DAILY REP. FOR EXECUTIVES (BNA), Feb. 26, 2002, *at* A-41 (ICANN's president argued for a $4.8 million current budget increase of 300 to 500 percent).

the involvement of the government in the organization so as to pressure the registries of the ccTLDs into signing contracts with ICANN, which would include an undertaking to pay. This move, which would increase governments' power, drew critics who were concerned with the possible reduced importance of other Internet constituencies,[65] and increased possible content control of the Internet.[66] Whether ICANN will raise its funding, however, is less clear, since even representatives of the government doubted the validity of the proposed expansion of ICANN's role in governing the Internet.[67] Thus, the use of governments to pressure the registries into signing the contracts did not seem to materialize. In fact, it may have backfired.

On the other hand, some highly dissatisfied registries threatened to leave ICANN altogether.[68] Others are examining the possibility of a new organization that would play a more active role in ICANN's governance, such as a Names Supporting Organization, which would be made up of representatives from the registries of the ccTLDs.[69]

5. Divide and Conquer

For a number of years, ICANN has attempted to reach an agreement with the registries of the ccTLDs on a form contract that they would sign. The attempt failed for a number of reasons. First, some individual registries rejected the particular provisions of the contracts, including significant payment obligations, without commensurate influence on the way in which the payments will be used. This was the "taxation without representation"

---

65   *See id.*

66   *See id.*

67   Juliana Gruenwald, *ICANN Board Meeting in Ghana to Focus on Structure as Private-Sector Driven Group,* DAILY REP. FOR EXECUTIVES (BNA), Mar. 13, 2002, *at* A-10 (concern expressed by "William Black, managing director of Nominet, which operates Britain's ccTLD, .uk, and chairman of a group of European ccTLD operators").

68   Stephen Joyce, *Worried About ICANN Responsiveness, ccTLD Managers Form New Support Group,* INT'L BUS. & FIN. DAILY (BNA), June 5, 2001, LEXIS, BNA Library, BNABUS File.

69   Juliana Gruenwald, *ICANN Board to Take Up Reform Plan Despite Concerns with Latest Proposal,* DAILY REP. FOR EXECUTIVES (BNA), June 25, 2002, *at* A-22. This possibility is now being considered by ICANN in its reorganization. The policy councils would include the address and numbering council, the generic top-level domain name policy council and the geographic top-level domain names council, including input from the ccTLD operators.

argument. Second, some governments may not have been pleased with ICANN's assertion of power over their ccTLDs, which the governments claimed to be their property. Other governments were not pleased with the assertion of ICANN's power over the registries of their country codes. Lastly, emotions and self-worth played a part. Registries did not seem to appreciate ICANN's letter to the government seeking assurance that the registries were qualified for the task.[70] Therefore, most registries did not sign.

ICANN then took the long road of negotiating with each registry separately. ICANN's President announced that agreements with operators of ccTLDs depend on the willingness of individual countries to accept ICANN's conditions. In other words, ICANN will not reduce its demands under the contracts. He conceded that the process will therefore take longer, but emphasized that ICANN is in no rush. "However, a member of the ccTLD Supporting Organization (ccTLD SO) told the board that relations between ICANN and the ccTLDs have not improved since he issued a warning about the problem at last year's annual meeting." "ICANN was insisting that ccTLDs agree that in the event of a change in registry, ccTLDs will facilitate the transfer to a successor nominated by ICANN (but) few countries would accept such a provision."[71]

The progress was indeed slow, but some progress was made. In 2002, ICANN reached an agreement with the registry of Japan's ccTLD. The registry agreed to recognize "ICANN's role in managing the Internet's domain name system" and to "provide financial support to ICANN and to operate the ccTLD in the 'interest of the Japanese community.'" ICANN promised to "ensure the stable and secure operation of the domain name system and to formally recognize the Japan Registry Service Corporation as the new operators of .jp."[72]

Few registries have signed such contracts. Initially, few registries signed such contracts, with many holding out for a greater role in the governance of the system, or lower fees or

---

70 *ICANN Intrigues—The Jonathan Cohen Interview—Part 2*, DEMYS NEWS SERVICE, Oct. 22, 2002, *formerly at* http://www.demys.net/news/2002/10/02_oct_22_icann_intrigues.htm (Oct. 22, 2002).

71 Tom Gilroy, *ICANN Expects Progress on ccTLDs, but No Surge of Agreements, President Says,* DAILY REP. FOR EXECUTIVES (BNA), Nov. 19, 2001, *at* A-6.

72 *ICANN Reaches Agreement with Operator of Japan's Country Code Top-Level Domain,* DAILY REP. FOR EXECUTIVES (BNA), Mar. 1, 2002, *at* A-42.

other more favorable conditions.[73] But they do not speak with one voice, and increasing numbers have signed contracts in the intervening years.[74] But they do not speak in one voice. "There are 240 ccTLDs, all of whom have different views . . . Some of them wanted to explore the option of what would happen if ICANN failed, and some of the more extreme ccTLDs put it in terms of leaving ICANN . . . "There's a whole lot of other end of the spectrum," . . . including constructive input on how to build the Country Code Names Supporting Organization (ccNSO)."[75] ICANN's powers and functions and the balance of power among the various constituencies are not settled as yet. The structure of the organization has been reformed recently, and is being further negotiated. In sum, ICANN is using the "divide and conquer" strategy while the registries and the governments have not formed a unified approach, but are nonetheless very reluctant to submit to ICANN's demands.

6. Arbitration

WIPO is interested in becoming the standard setter (and perhaps bearer) on some of the issues concerning ccTLDs, and so are many governments. WIPO, urged on by Argentina, Canada, Denmark, France, the U.S. and the EU, has drawn up a code of "best practices" for use by ccTLD administrators to resolve domain name disputes,[76] and has been involved in resolving numerous such disputes.[77] Furthermore, dozens of countries have voluntary arrangements with WIPO to handle disputes using their country

---

73   ICANN, *ccTLD Agreements,* at http://www.icann.org/cctlds/agreements. html (providing links to the twelve agreements that ccTLD registries have with ICANN) (last updated Oct. 31, 2023).

74   See multiple files entitled "ICANN Formalizes Relationship with ccTLD Manager for _____," with individual files for Brazil, Panama, Ukraine, Guatemala, Egypt, Tajikistan, Netherlands, Senegal, Thailand, and others.

75   Cheryl Bolen, *ICANN Board Moves Forward on Reform, Setting Stage for Next Meeting, Lynn Says,* Antitrust & Trade Reg. Daily (BNA), Nov. 1, 2002, LEXIS, BNA Library, BNABUS File.

76   WIPO, *ccTLD Best Practices for the Prevention and Resolution of Intellectual Property Disputes* (June 20, 2001), *at* http://arbiter.wipo.int/domains/cctld/ bestpractices/bestpractices.html; Daniel Pruzin, *WIPO to Consider Consultations on Cybersquatting, Other Domain Abuses,* 17 Int'l Trade Rep. (BNA), July 13, 2000, *at* 1071.

77   *See* https://www.wipo.int/amc/en/index.html (last visited Aug. 22, 2023). *See generally* WIPO UDRP Domain Name Cases, *at* https://arbiter.wipo.int/ domains/cases/all-cctld.html (last visited Aug. 5, 2004).

codes.[78] WIPO members such as the United States and the EU are keen to see "best practice" codes put into place for other countries to contain the scourge of cybersquatting. One school of thought is that now that there is this quick and effective procedure against cybersquatting in the gTLDs, a lot of cybersquatting activity will move to the ccTLDs.[79]

Other international organizations, such as the ITU, are also vying for the position of a "negotiation platform manager." The ITU has been serving for many years in a similar capacity for postal services. Arguably, ICANN has not done better than any bureaucratic organization in terms of time, especially with respect to policy matters. In addition, the ITU serves as a mediator for standard setting rather than as a standard-setting power. This approach is in line with the rapidly evolving development of the Internet. However, the ITU does not enable the United States to maintain its current power position as the ICANN structure does. The role of the ITU may be shaped in the future, but it is not likely to play the same current role it plays in the postal service context.

7. The Relationship Between the United States and ICANN Mirrors a Non-Zero-Sum Game

Neither party wishes to sever the relationship. Although the United States, which in the final analysis controls ICANN by its contract with the Department of Commerce, desires to keep the final control over the root, it also desires the control to be in the form of monitoring rather than overt directives. United States law precludes the Department of Commerce from controlling ICANN, unless ICANN is reestablished by statute. However, the Department of Commerce does have the power to terminate ICANN's contract. The Department is sensitive to dissatisfactions with ICANN. It can therefore make additional demands on ICANN to correct its operations or shorten its contract term.

Further, like the couple in the hypothetical, we witness changes in events that tend to press for cooperation rather than competition. The United States, which had full control over the root, tied its own hands by avoiding the creation of an ICANN-

---

78   *See* WIPO, *Domain Name Dispute Resolution Service for Country Code Top Level Domains* (ccTLDs), *formerly at* http://arbiter.wipo.int/domains/cctld/index.html (Oct. 30, 2023), *now see* https://www.wipo.int/amc/en/index.html (last visited Aug. 22, 2023).

79   Daniel Pruzin, *WIPO to Consider Consultations on Cybersquatting, Other Domain Abuses*, 17 INT'L TRADE REP. (BNA), July 13, 2000, *at* 1071.

type corporation under a statute. Had the United States chosen this route, it would have had the power to control and manage ICANN to a far greater degree. But by creating a non-government corporation, it has legally limited its own power to manage ICANN. Nonetheless, by contract, it has reserved the ultimate power to itself, and the ability to influence ICANN by possessing the power (threat) not to renew the contract. Today, the United States uses its power to avoid conflicts with other governments and powerful actors. Since the United States has changed its mind and no longer promises to release ICANN from its ties to the government, a consistent approach or sensitivity to the other governments is necessary to help gain the trust of other actors and establish a pattern of cooperation.

Whether this pattern will continue is unclear. It would seem that so long as this ambiguous status satisfies the interests of the United States and can be used to satisfy the interests and demands of other governments, ICANN will continue to exist. Changes will be made within ICANN in terms of balance of power, identity of actors and participants, and processes. The chances of creating a new structure altogether seem to be low unless the whole naming system finds another form.

Each of the players in the naming system may have established a "minimum-maximum strategy" that dictates how far the player will go either in its demands or in giving in to the demands of the other players. For example, it seems that the minimum demands of the United States are to control the geographical place of the root and the legal arrangement with the organizations that manage the root. The maximum demand is probably close to the minimum, and the range is minimal. For the United States the current flexible situation seems to be ideal. From the point of view of other governments, their minimum demands are further removed from their maximum demands. One main reason is the dependence on the United States' largess and fairness, or dependence on the United States no matter how fair it might behave. But as long as the United States has made it clear that it will not relinquish control, and as long as it accommodates the minimal strategic demands of the other governments, cooperation is likely to continue and the status quo will be changed only in small steps of "muddling through."

I. *The Platform for Negotiations: Why Are Governments Interested in ICANN As a Platform for Negotiation?*

ICANN can develop into a platform for negotiation. This platform can develop into a central power, slowly building a power base through negotiations that put it at the center as a pivotal necessary party, like the central pole in a carousel. The pole is useless by itself, but all other important parts are tied to it and depend on it for balance, support and function. However, if the crucial parties bypass ICANN, and if the distance between them is not great, ICANN may lose its pivotal power. For example, if the United States and representatives of governments negotiate directly within the government committee, then ICANN's staff and board would have to carry out the agreements among the governments, but would have little say in these agreements. Currently, it seems that for many reasons that should be explored further, the governments prefer to go through ICANN's personnel and board, even though they also deal with each other directly and have the option of using other organizations to get in touch with each other, including the GAC appended to ICANN.

It seems that the registries of ccTLDs are being organized in order to have a special say in ICANN. For example, the Number Resource Organization ("NRO") formed in late 2003 to coordinate efforts by regional Internet registries in dealing with ICANN.[80] They may also become the voice of the governments whose countries they serve. It may be that each country will develop some partial naming system and, perhaps, that some countries may band together to create regional naming systems that would not impede the overall naming system but rather reduce its importance. Even though it seems that ICANN is going in that direction, I do not believe that ICANN will end up as a power center.

If ICANN evolves into a platform for negotiations to augment its power rather than to attain a consensus, a far more serious problem will arise both for ICANN, and indirectly for the United States. There are international organizations that are far more apt and have far more experience at reaching consensus. On the other hand, few organizations involved in ICANN's infrastructure, including governments and ccTLDs, are likely to

---

80 *NRO, The Number Resource Organization (NRO)*, https://www.nro.net/about/ (Oct. 30, 2023); *see* https://www.nro.net/about/history-of-the-nro/ (both last visited Oct. 30, 2023) (proposed Memorandum of Understanding).

participate in an authoritarian organization, unless they control it. As the conflicts between ccTLDs and ICANN sharpen, and given ICANN's unwillingness to police itself, there is a growing pressure to move to other actors. However, the United States has a stake in keeping ICANN, and its own control of ICANN, alive. Hence, it has pressured ICANN to become more transparent and has shortened its contract period.

J. Lessons From the Bargains or Lack Thereof

With respect to the weaker parties, such as some registries and many registrars, who are lower in the power hierarchy, ICANN has been successful in reaching agreements that fit its preferences. Whether or not these agreements fit the preferences of the weaker parties, the weaker parties likely concluded that they would be better off with these agreements than without them. Thus, the equilibrium between ICANN and such parties has been established, and may be described as the rule for parties of this ilk. However, ICANN does not seem to consider these parties as a sufficient source of funding, nor as the foundation of power. Early on, ICANN attempted to impose a relatively small charge on each domain name holder. However, the negative reaction to this attempt from Congress and other significant competitors to ICANN's power caused a quick withdrawal of this proposal. Thus, these parties are not generally ICANN's power competitors. They are not organized and do not have the national or international clout necessary to induce ICANN to change its position. Therefore, it makes sense for ICANN to focus on the registries of the ccTLDs as a source of funding, and on the governments as a foundation of power or the source of funding or the party able to pressure the ccTLDs to be more generous with their payments.

ICANN was not successful in reaching an agreement with the organized group of ccTLD registries. They objected to the contract provision that bound them to future policy decisions, that is, to the assertion of power, and they did not consider ICANN's services sufficient consideration for the payments they were making and were required to make. In consideration for these two concessions, they demanded greater power of participation in the decisions that would affect them. ICANN did not agree to meet these demands and chose the strategy described above. The registries are also not of one mind, and the chances are that some will defect and sign a negotiated contract, while others will hold out for more.

The Department of Commerce has also initially reduced its support of ICANN by renewing its contract for a shorter period in 2002,[81] while Congress held hearings that allowed criticisms of ICANN to be heard from witnesses, including the General Accounting Office, as well as members of the Congressional committee.

In September 2003, the Department of Commerce extended the agreement for another three years. The Department stated that "[w]hile numerous issues and substantial challenges confront ICANN, the organization has made notable progress toward achieving the goals of the (agreement) in the start-up phase of its existence," and noted that "the agreement included 'key' provisions to ensure that ICANN developed into an independent, stable and sustainable organization capable of technically managing the domain name system." The Department noted ICANN's recent reforms but said that "much work remains."[82]

There is no strategic consensus among ICANN's main power holders: the governments, the ccTLD registries, the United States Department of Commerce and the Congressional committee in charge of monitoring the naming system. Not all believe that their strategy is optimal. However, there is another lack of equilibrium that strengthens ICANN's power—the disagreement between the United States and other foreign countries with respect to the control of the root. There is no consensus among the European Union, other countries, and the United States with respect to the "internationalization" of the root and the extent to which the

---

81 *Internet Oversight Body Wins One More Year of Life,* Deseret News (Salt Lake City, Utah), Sept. 21, 2002, *at* B10, LEXIS, News Library, AllNews File (noting that the Department granted a one-year renewal—until Sept. 30, 2003—the third renewal of the contract). The Department expressed disappointment in ICANN's progress on the contract tasks but "consider(ed) the organization's recent broad reform efforts to be a substantial justification for affording ICANN a limited amount of time to achieve the (contract) tasks."

82 *Agencies,* Wash. Internet Daily, Sept. 18, 2003, LEXIS, News Library, AllNews File. The agreement includes "milestones" for ICANN, including a new strategic plan by the end of the year, a contract audit compliance program by June 30, and a contingency plan in the event of a severe disruption of its operations. ICANN also is required to continue seeking agreements with ccTLD operators and to implement, by December 31, 2004, an appropriate long-term strategy for selecting new TLDs.

United States should control the root.[83] Any fundamental change in ICANN's identity may allow for an open reconsideration of the power position of the United States. As long as ICANN's function as the guardian and manager of the root is not on the negotiation table, the United States' utility is met. That, however, allows the United States to negotiate, through ICANN, its behavior or processes or even the extent of its power. For example, there is no reason why ICANN should determine issues concerning control of information. There are other bodies, both in the United States and in other countries, that can determine these issues and there is no need for uniformity—at least no immediate need—on this score.

We can, therefore, expect the United States to continue to maintain ICANN, to be sensitive to the demands of the other countries, and to curb ICANN's ambitions. The United States can afford, and has the ability, by contract, to limit ICANN's desires to acquire centralized discretionary control over anything that might possibly relate to the Internet naming and numbering system, and to use this ever-expanding control and operations as a source of ever-expanding funding. To be sure, an idealistic view of ICANN is unrealistic. It does not make ICANN better and stronger. But then, there are some people and institutions that would not wish ICANN to be stronger. In their opinion the weaker it is, the better it will be.

The tension and the bargaining areas are likely to center not on finding alternatives to ICANN. They are likely to focus on defining ICANN's power, weakening its appetite for establishing policies, and limiting its budget. In that area, the United States and other countries may reach an agreement, which ICANN will be forced to follow. If, however, the United States and the other countries insist on their demands for controlling the root in terms of geography and servicers, they may be forced into the existing equilibrium and into far greater threats that would be far more costly to each in attempting to win.

One last possibility that looms in the background of this saga is the development of an alternative naming system that would be more suitable to the Internet of today and tomorrow. There are scientists that are working on such a system, and when this is achieved, the problems of the present will be those of the

---

83 *See, e.g.,* Monika Ermert, *Speakers Seek Full Internationalization of ICANN During WSIS Panel,* WASH. INTERNET DAILY, Mar. 5, 2004, LEXIS, News Library, AllNews File.

past; ICANN may become entirely obsolete, and new problems are likely to emerge. Unlike new fuel, whose introduction might require massive capital investments, and cause the obsolescence of an enormous amount of existing investments, a change in the naming system will involve very little of each in terms of money but much more, perhaps, in terms of knowledge. But if the knowledge can be acquired while the people in control remain in control, the transition may be far easier and more acceptable.

II.   CONCLUSION

While ICANN was hailed as a new design, and to some extent it is, there is nothing fundamentally new about it, except that it has not yet matured. Every governance model contains flexibility as well as structure. From free markets[84] to the most rigid dictatorship, some actions are left to the actors and are not prescribed from above. It seems that even chaotic systems have some structures, such as fractals.[85] The governance of the Internet naming system has not yet found the balance between structure and flexibility, between principles upon which people negotiate and negotiations where "anything goes" depending on muscle and wile. There is no balance as yet between strategic techniques designed to gain advantages for the parties (usually short-term) and a long-term view of the ultimate goals of the organization. There is little balance between a self-limiting approach to power as opposed to a drive for expansion of power, between the imposition of uniformity and "best practices" and room for individual and organizational experiments.

Do the issues discussed in this paper indicate a potential for developing patterns of behavior that can materialize as rules governing all parties involved in the naming system, or even the rules governing the relationships between governments and their registries? As long as the parties depend on ICANN, and as long

---

84   Tamar Frankel, *The Legal Infrastructure of Markets: The Role of Contract and Property Law,* 73 B.U.L. REV. 389 (1993).

85   *See, e.g.,* Michael J. Martinez, *Fractals Flowing Online, formerly at* http:// abcnews.go.com/sections/tech/CuttingEdge/fractals990316.html (last visited Feb. 13, 2003) (noting the identification of structures (fractals) within the chaotic system of the Internet information transfer and working on using these fractals to build mathematical models that would help predict the behavior of this chaotic system and gain efficiencies); Adam J. Pearson, Words from the Wind, *at* https://philosophadam.wordpress.com/2011/11/20/fractals-and-the-structure-of-reality/ (last visited Dec. 24, 2023).

as their relationship with ICANN is established by contracts or by participation in some related organization, the odds of rules evolving are quite slim. Each of these forms allows for negotiations rather than consensus-building. Nonetheless, it seems that some conclusions can be reached with respect to the relationships between governments and their registries.

The governments and the registries are likely to agree on a relationship without much interference by ICANN. That is because ICANN's power over the relationships is limited to changes in the identity of the delegates who operate the ccTLDs. If the delegates are government organizations, then the changes in personnel will hardly ever be subject to ICANN's interference. As between the parties, it is very likely that the emerging rules will grant the governments full power over the ccTLDs. The governments' stronger position at ICANN, their close relationships with the U.S. Department of State, and their deeper commitment to their country names, suggest that the registries would become legally, or in reality, the governments' agents. The Australian experience suggests that the registries' status as private professionals offering public service is giving way to a far more controlled status in the service of the countries' political and business interests. Unless the registries could organize and establish a countervailing power at ICANN, and perhaps even if they succeed in doing so, they will not be able to overcome the strong pressure of national governments to comply with the governments' policies.

The real conflict, which is currently relatively latent, will arise when the governments demand "internationalization" of the Internet in terms of language and staffing of ICANN. The real conflict seems to be between the governments and the United States. If the United States values the control of the root, it may have to reduce ICANN's powers over this task, and agree that other matters will be determined by one or more organizations. For example, the ITU could provide a platform for negotiations among governments and other constituencies, while technical organizations can perform the technical services that ICANN currently performs through the same organizations as independent contractors.

The important questions remain: will the current style of contract negotiations for private laws lead to a more predictable governance structure? Will this system gain wide acceptance, legitimacy and respect? Or will this style lead to the production of "private laws" that depend on the power balance of the parties and the pressures of outside parties at the particular time?

THE MANAGING LAWMAKER IN CYBERSPACE: A NEW POWER MODEL

THE MANAGING LAWMAKER IN CYBERSPACE: A NEW POWER MODEL*

Tamar Frankel

I. INTRODUCTION

This Article is about power—the ability to gain obedience whether by captivating followers, persuading skeptics or awarding and withdrawing economic benefits. The purpose of this Article is to analyze how the power of the Internet Corporation for Names and Numbers ("ICANN") was created, augmented, strengthened and reined in. Many controversies surround ICANN, including the very foundation of its existence—the need for a single "root" in the Internet naming infrastructure—its organizational form and accountability, and the utterances, policies and actions of its management.

The purpose of this Article is not to argue and prescribe but to describe and explain. Description, however, is rarely, if ever, neutral. This Article is no exception. The author is biased in favor of the ICANN experiment. I hope it matures to become a model for a global organization—with a limited mission, grounded in a unique type of consensus, and operated in a special kind of balance of power environment. I hope that ICANN's processes and activities will reflect the spirit of the Internet that it influences. I hope that it will exercise its power only to address problems when they arise, and nurture innovation whenever possible. I hope that the Internet community and ICANN will follow the "rule of

---

* Tamar Frankel, *The Managing Lawmaker in Cyberspace: A Power Model*, 27 BROOK. J. INT'L L. 859 (2002), *available at* https://brooklynworks.brooklaw.edu/bjil/vol27/iss3/16. Reprinted with permission from the Brooklyn Journal of International Law.

I owe many of the clarifications in this paper to comments of David Johnson, Esq., Kenneth A. Cukier, Editor, Wall Street Journal, Asia, Hong Kong, and Professor Michael Meuer, Boston University Law School.

consensus" just as civil societies follow the rule of law. Events in the past month are perhaps bringing the issues to a head, but at this stage my crystal ball is dim and hope reigns supreme.

ICANN operates in a dual capacity: as a manager and a lawmaker. It provides high-level management of some of the Internet's operational infrastructure. I use the term management in a very broad sense. ICANN neither operates nor fully controls any of the actors that constitute the Internet's infrastructure. It has, however, power, in varied degrees, to direct these actors.[1] For lack of a better word, I call this direction "managing." In addition, ICANN establishes some of the Internet's constitutive rules that facilitate universal connectivity.[2] It has used its power to determine the process under which new top-level domain names ("TLDs") are allocated. To this extent it is a lawmaker.

The inquiry into ICANN is important because ICANN plays a significant role in the operation of the Internet. The inquiry is interesting because, like the Internet, ICANN has no precise analog.[3] The inquiry is difficult because the location and identity of ICANN's power is murky, contradictory and confusing. Its power structure is fashioned after a private not-for-profit corporation, but it does not operate an enterprise that such a corporation usually operates, like a museum, hospital or a membership organization of credit card issuers. ICANN's operations involve an enigma—the Internet—which defies a clear analogy. The Internet has been defined as: a new world community; the foundation

---

1   ICANN's power over the Internet service providers ("ISPs") is minimal, and depends on their consensus of using a single root. Its power over the registries of most country code top-level domain names is limited, but it can exert more pressure on registries of generic top-level domain names. *See infra* Part II.A.1-2.

2   ICANN plays a lesser role with respect to ISPs. Large ISPs can decide whether to point at the ICANN root. They have no contractual obligation to follow ICANN's policies, or otherwise interact with ICANN except in connection with the allocation of intellectual property blocks.

3   Some international organizations, such as the International Olympic Commission and the Diamond Exchange, have arisen not by the support of governments or laws, but through the initiative of participants. Similar initiatives have given rise to national organizations, such as stock exchanges, trade organizations and professional associations. However, they differ from ICANN in a number of important aspects. They were organized directly by the interested parties; their purpose of organization was usually quite specific (such as the Olympic Games) or for the purpose of regulating their members, and most national organizations are regulated by governments, who serve as backup regulators.

of democracy; a communication system; a form of commerce; a network of networks; and a novel technology. Each definition brings an analogy to relationships and power structures. It has been suggested that new technologies undergo a process of chaos and finally settle at something close to familiar models, with some adjustments.[4] I believe that this thesis is correct, and that what we see today is a stage in the evolutionary process of the Internet and its infrastructure. However, the road to the ultimate adjusted model may determine its choice. The road to ICANN's final model may be less bumpy if the model reflects the characteristics of the Internet. I believe that the Internet is closer to a market. Therefore, I analogize ICANN to a manager of a unique type of market.

The use of the market image for the Internet and its infrastructure may seem counterintuitive. More often, ICANN's image is drawn from the store of political metaphors as a global government, and its users as citizens; the relationship among users, service providers and ICANN is thereby grounded in a "social contract." Markets and political units share some features. Both require an infrastructure and an implicit agreement—a consensus—among most actors as to the fundamental "rules of the game." Mainly, these rules are born of a rule of consensus, which people follow even if they are free not to do so. A "social contract" governs many aspects of our lives, and so do the markets on which we draw for the essentials for living and for earning our livelihood. The distinction, therefore, between the two is not in impact but perhaps in the enforcement power. The markets' coercive powers are more limited. Yet concern for the integrity of the system (whether the political or economic system) drives many dissenters on details to adhere to the general rules of the majority. It seems that the main difference is in the kinds of enforcement tools that markets can use. In that respect, ICANN's enforcement tools resemble those of the markets and not those of the political units.

I believe that even though ICANN's objectives and powers have not yet been fully defined, its analog is closer to the New York Stock Exchange, Inc. ("NYSE") than to a civil society. ICANN's foundation is grounded in technical and business practices, the objectives of its social contract are limited, and it lacks coercive state power. Therefore, I stick to my market model. But because

---

4   *See* Debora L. Spar, RULING THE WAVES 11-22 (2001).

the Internet affects social interaction, and because it is evolving, I admit to ICANN's political undertones.[5]

Perhaps because of ICANN's political aspects, the Internet market and ICANN differ from the securities markets and their managing lawmakers. ICANN and the actors constituting the infrastructure of the Internet are essentially unregulated.[6] Their accountability to a "higher authority," such as the Department of Commerce ("DOC"), is unclear. Even the authority of the DOC is subject to queries. Moreover, ICANN functions partly as a policy setting institution, partly as a platform for negotiation and mediation. ICANN has not yet reached maturity, and is likely to operate in a state of flexible adjustment for some time to come. Recent events suggest that the state of flux may also turn into a state of shocks, counter shocks, restructure and substitution.

ICANN poses a number of puzzles. First, it is essentially an unregulated and undemocratic natural monopoly. It is managing and making rules for a hierarchical system that, in the view of experts, cannot be governed by two entities efficiently. Yet ICANN's power at its inception was quite weak. How can a monopoly be weak? Is not a weak monopoly a contradiction in terms?

5   I do not analogize ICANN to the United Nations or its organizations, first because UN membership is usually limited to political units, while ICANN was explicitly designed to exclude the control, though not the influence, of such units. In addition, the UN's decisions can be backed by force, while it is doubtful whether ICANN's will ever have such a backing. *See* Nancy C.M. Hartsock, Money, Sex, and Power 55 (1983) (dealing with economic markets, noting the disparities among the actors and arguing that the market model legitimizes domination by the strong actors over the weaker actors). ICANN can be analogized to the NYSE. Both institutions act as a focal point and as a synthesizer among the disparate parts that constitute the infrastructure of a system. Both pass rules affecting the infrastructure of the markets. ICANN deals with the domain name registries and the registrars, and to some extent influences the ISPs. The NYSE deals with the underwriters, brokers and dealers. Both Internet actors and securities market actors operate independently, some for profit and some not for profit. Both the NYSE and ICANN combine management and lawmaking. Both have a board of directors, officers and employees who carry out institutional functions. Both are in the public eye, for all to see and judge. Like the New York brokers who gathered on the curb in the late eighteenth century, ICANN's creators started by interacting and searching for a network communication unlimited by subject matter and purposes.

6   ICANN is a not-for-profit corporation incorporated under the laws of California. However, the regulatory scope of both laws and enforcers of laws is very limited. *See* ICANN, Articles of Incorporation (1998), *available at* https://www.icann.org/general/articles.htm (last visited Sept. 6, 2023).

Part II of this Article addresses this query. After a brief description of the basic structure of the Internet naming and numbering system relevant to ICANN's power, Part II describes the unique circumstances under which ICANN was created to explain its weak initial existence. ICANN's power was and remains a default power. There were many candidates for managing and controlling ICANN's functions. All vied for the position. But no candidate agreed that any of the others would take control of the entity. ICANN's power stemmed from the consensus by the parties that none of them would control. ICANN was not vested with power. It came into being by the grace of powerful constituencies that refrained from asserting their power. Hence, ICANN's weakness.

A second puzzle follows. While ICANN started weak, it has managed to become far stronger. How could this weak monopoly become stronger with time? Part III of this Article offers an answer. ICANN has maintained and strengthened its following by strongly supporting the stability of the Internet (standardizing the infrastructure). This prime directive of maintaining stability is of great concern to almost everyone around the globe. In addition, ICANN's staff has taken special care to ensure that none of the potential claimants to ICANN's control would be sufficiently displeased to attempt to wrench control over it. The staff solved problems through mediation. Other events and external parties helped. ICANN has flexed its muscles in exercising the powers clearly vested in it, that is, allocating the valuable right to operate TLDs. ICANN has augmented its power through a stable and able management, including the preparation of its contracts, which contain significant powers. This staff has steered ICANN through the turbulent waters of complex international and national laws, supervised its statements and negotiated on its behalf. Part III of this Article offers a few examples that demonstrate ICANN's rising power.

However, in the past month, ICANN's staff proposed to restructure the institution. The new structure would eliminate some of the constraints under which the staff was operating, expand the staff and offer more powerful positions to constituents that would finance ICANN and its expansion.[7] The proposal would establish tighter control and greater power for ICANN

---

7   *See* ICANN, PRESIDENT'S REPORT: ICANN–THE CASE FOR REFORM (2002), *at* https://www.icann.org/general/lynn-reform-proposal-24feb02.htm (last visited Sept. 6, 2023).

and its staff, a self-perpetuating board representing the strong constituencies with vested interests in the Internet and lower input by the unorganized public.

The proposal seems to have been approved by some constituencies, but has prompted protests by others and raised questions in Congress (although ICANN's restructure is not one of the main topics in Congress today). The result of these protests is unclear. Short-term, the staff may ignore them: the proposal may be a basis for negotiation and some "softening." Long-term, if controls tighten and public input shrinks, some predict a cessation of some parts of the infrastructure and perhaps a temporary split of the Internet.[8] These developments support the explanation of ICANN's rising powers.

A third puzzle that ICANN poses relates to its current status. While it has flexed its muscles and become stronger, its exercise of power has been fairly contained. Since ICANN is a natural monopoly that has become stronger with time, what has prevented it in the past, and what prevents it today, from taking a far more high-handed and extensive ruling posture?

Part IV of this Article deals with this question. The emergence of ICANN, its staying power, and the limitations on the exercise of its power can be partly explained by an analogy to the economic theory of "contestable markets."[9] The theory deals with price. I equate price to power. High prices denote a high level of power. Low prices denote a lower level of power. The theory of

---

8   See A. Michael Froomkin, *Wrong Turn in Cyberspace: Using ICANN to Route Around the APA and the Constitution*, 50 Duke L.J. 17, 181-82 (2000).

9   See William J. Baumol et al., Contestable Markets and The Theory of Industry Structure 5 (1982). The authors state:

We define a perfectly contestable market as one that is accessible to potential entrants and has the following two properties: First, the potential entrants can, without restriction, serve the same market demands and use the same productive techniques as those available to the incumbent firms. Thus, there are no entry barriers in the sense of the term used by Stigler. Second, the potential entrants evaluate the profitability of entry at the incumbent firms' pre-entry prices. That is, although the potential entrants recognize that an expansion of industry outputs leads to lower prices—in accord with the market demand curves—the entrants nevertheless assume that if they undercut incumbents' prices they can sell as much of the corresponding good as the quantity demanded by the market at their own prices. *Id.* "Stigler defines an entry barrier to be present when the potential entrants face costs greater than those incurred (by the incumbent)." *Id.*

contestable markets suggests that in some cases a monopolist (or an oligopolist) will charge the low price it would have charged had the market been competitive. These are the cases in which the monopolist is more efficient than its potential competitors, and can therefore sell or service at lower prices. At these prices, the less efficient competitors would not enter the market.[10]

Yet the monopolist will not raise the prices in contestable markets. In these markets, entry costs for potential competitors would not be higher than the entry costs for the monopolist.[11] For example, the cost of airplanes for two airlines will be close, if not identical. In addition, the exit costs for competitors would be zero or close to zero.[12] Thus, the theory predicts that competitors will not enter the market only so long as they cannot afford to charge the monopolist's low prices. If, however, the monopolist charges higher prices, competitors will enter the market to offer the same service at the same prices or lower. When prices fall, these competitors will pocket their profits and exit the markets. This theory suggests that the "potential or threatened competition of possible new competitors" presents a great constraining force.[13]

---

10   For example, if one airline provides an optimal service between two towns (e.g., twice a week), and charges a price that allows it minimal profits, no competing airline will choose the same route. Another example is traditional securities underwriting, which involves high risks and requires very high investment and a distribution system. Smaller broker dealers did not enter this market because they could not compete with the very large underwriters on price and reliable performance. Among the underwriters there exists an apex structure. In 1983, the structure was predicted to continue, and it seems in 2001 that it has. *See* Samuel L. Hayes III et al., Competition in the Investment Banking Industry 72-73, 76 (1983). The authors note research which suggests that "investment banking has long tended to assume a pyramidal competitive structure, with a few preeminent firms providing leadership in both financing and collateral services" and a tendency towards increased concentration. *Id.* at 78. Nonetheless, the authors argue that this structure "masks a competitive structure" because the markets are segmented. *Id.* "[C]ertain types of clients and industries tend to gravitate towards (certain types of investment bankers)." *Id.* at 79.

11   *See* William J. Baumol et al., Contestable Markets and The Theory of Industry Structure 7 (1982) (stating the airline industry as an example).

12   For example, an airline can exit a route with little cost by redirecting its planes to another route.

13   William J. Baumol et al., Contestable Markets and The Theory of Industry Structure 13 (1982).

Potential competition will "extend the beneficent sway of the invisible hand" that leads the market.[14]

The theory of contestable markets highlights a special "balance of power" and its restraining effect. I believe that a similar idea of a contestable market helps us understand ICANN's environment. To be sure, while its institutional structure is still evolving, ICANN's existence and activities are based on a consensus among numerous power holders. More importantly, the large Internet service providers' ("ISPs") consensus to use a single root constitutes the foundation of ICANN's power. Most importantly, the tugging pressure of "path dependence" in the case of ICANN is very great. It costs to change legacy-systems. A move by some and not by other participants of the infrastructure may endanger the universality and integrity of the Internet. Even a slight move may generate a slippery slope towards disorder and unpredictability. The beneficent principle of "the devil you know" engenders an almost knee-jerk reaction in this case. Nonetheless, I believe that the need for one guiding hand—a natural monopoly, on the one hand, and the ability of some players to overthrow ICANN or particular actions of ICANN, as illuminated by the theory of contestable markets—limits ICANN's exercise of power.

The recent proposal to restructure ICANN supports the thesis of this Article.[15] Under the proposal, public representation on ICANN's board has been eliminated. Five of the nine directors' seats reserved for representatives of the public were allocated to representatives of governments—each seat to be occupied by a representative of a world region.[16] Arguably, the governments

---

14   The theory of contestable markets has led to the deregulation of the airlines, among others. Deregulation, however, demonstrated the flaws in the theory's predictions. The *correct* monopolistic or competitive price absent actual competition is controversial. Entry barriers defined as "sunken costs" are difficult to determine. It was discovered that exit involves transaction costs. Further, there is a price lag that provides insufficient after-entry profits for the entering competitors during the "hit-and-run" period. All these issues require correction, but judicial or government correction increases costs, and small corrections may result in far larger deviations. Thus, application of the theory is far from perfect. *See* William B. Tye, THE THEORY OF CONTESTABLE MARKETS (1990) (listing a number of flaws in the theory).

15   *See* ICANN, PRESIDENT'S REPORT: ICANN–THE CASE FOR REFORM (2002), *at* https://www.icann.org/general/lynn-reform-proposal-24feb02.htm   (last visited Sept. 6, 2023).

16   *Id.*

are the effective representatives of the people.[17] Each of the other representations will be selected by a particular powerful constituency. One reason for the change seems to be ICANN's management's concern with ICANN's financing. Specifically, the management desired to finance the expansion of ICANN's activities and its staff. The governments will finance, but obtain a stronger voice in ICANN's governing body. It seems that the European Union will also gain ICANN's support for its new country code top-level domain name ("ccTLD"), ".eu," as an exception to the practice that only United Nations recognized countries be awarded this type of name. Thus, the potential competitors of ICANN joined it and presumably would compete or negotiate inside rather than outside the organization. A consensus among the constituents will make ICANN a very strong monopoly because the ranks of the constraining outside forces will dwindle. That development may ultimately pose a danger to the integrity of the Internet. A strong and authoritarian ICANN may become a true regulator that departs from the spirit and loose structure of the Internet. That may press dissidents to combine, build and offer an alternative, which is technically feasible even today. Today, such an alternative does not draw members of the infrastructure. If ICANN tightens the reins sufficiently to strengthen the dissidents, an alternative will gain followers, or the dissidents may gain control, "capture" ICANN, and the experiment will continue.

A less prominent aspect of the contestable markets theory is the interest of all competing parties in maintaining a viable market. If competition drives the consumers away altogether, or destroys the market structure, the competitors have nothing to compete for.[18] One of the main objectives of the parties interested in the Internet is to ensure a thriving Internet. Control by itself is insufficient unless the Internet is preserved. The binding force of all parties today is the belief that the Internet will not survive unless it has a single root. Parties with a stake in the continued operation of the Internet are very reluctant to enter into a competing structure that may endanger the Internet's inter-operability. This is the glue that holds all participants together. On this issue the rule of consensus

---

17   Governments were excluded from the board under the current structure. They did, however, participate as an advisory committee. The proposed restructure would include government representatives as directors.

18   Thus, competitors will not use violence to compete (plant bombs at each other's shops) because the marketplace becomes too dangerous to visit and consumers will avoid all shops.

is imperative. But if a new technology develops in which one or more alternative roots do not disrupt the smooth operation of the Internet, then ICANN's power will become meaningless or far weaker than its controllers currently aim. They will then grasp at nothing, just as they cannot grasp today at some parts of the Internet's infrastructure that are not dependent on the single root concept. Even though the probability that this alternative will be effective seems very low, its effect is drastic. Therefore, pressure to develop and build alternatives to the single root may be another constraining element in the Internet power market.

This Article concludes that ICANN's power is still being shaped. It could emerge along a market model, as a central catalyst for consensus building among parties with different interests. ICANN would address problems as they arise. This model would also be closer to the model that the technical community follows, although money is not its mover. In a previous draft of this Article, I suggested that "[a]lternatively, ICANN could also move towards a more regulatory model based on the consensus of powerful constituencies who have a significant stake in ICANN." It seems that the current restructuring attempt of ICANN's management moves toward this model. Or ICANN can combine the two models to form a more structured market and more flexible regulatory body. Or none of these governance models would make a difference. A new ICANN, an alternative system or no system may rise by a technology that is today a mere twinkle in someone's eye.

II. A Puzzle: How Can a Natural Monopoly Be Weak?

A. ICANN Manages a Hierarchical System that Is a Natural Monopoly

As everyone knows, the Internet can be viewed as a network of networks free of central control and led by an "invisible hand." That is true to an extent, just as markets can be viewed as interactions among individuals and groups free of central control. To this extent, both systems are led by an invisible hand. Both, however, cannot function without an infrastructure.[19] Put in biblical terms, without a common language, both systems can become a dysfunctional Tower of Babel. The current Internet

---

19   *See* Tamar Frankel, *The Legal Infrastructure of Markets: The Role of Contract and Property Law*, 73 B.U.L. Rev. 389 (1993).

network structure requires that each receiver and sender of messages will have a unique one-of-a-kind designation, and that each computer message will have a unique number so that the "packages" of transported information will reach their destination.[20] The design further requires that transmissions be governed by acceptable protocols. If receivers, senders or spaces do not have unique designations and if the actors serving as the infrastructure do not follow the protocols, messages will miss their destinations. The Internet will become the Tower of Babel.[21]

1. The Feudal Structure of the Naming and Numbering Systems

With a view to preventing chaos and ensuring stability, the Internet naming and numbering system was designed in a hierarchical mode. Each level contains a signifier, under which names and numbers within its sphere of influence are recorded. The single root or dot (".") is in fact a database for two letter country code domain names such as ".uk" (United Kingdom) or ".fr" (France). The single root zone also contains generic top-level domain names ("gTLDs"), such as ".com," ".org," ".gov" and ".edu."[22] That system ensures, for example, that no other ".edu"

20 *See, e.g.*, Milton Mueller, *Technology and Institutional Innovation: Internet Domain Names*, 5 Int'l. J. Comm. L. & Pol'y 1 (2000), *available at* https://ciaotest.cc.columbia.edu/olj/ijclp/ijclp_5/ijclp_5a.pdf (last visited Dec. 22, 2023).

21 *See* Internet Architecture Board, Technical Comment on the Unique DNS Root (1999), *at* https://www.icann.org/correspondence/iab-tech-comment-27sept99.htm (last visited Sept. 2023) (stating that information emphasizing the current one root should remain intact to avoid confusion within the Internet community); James Middleton, *ICANN Tackles "Alternative" Domain Names*, Vnunet.com (June 1, 2001), *formerly at* http://www.vnunet.com/News/1122310 (the author notes "rogue domains" and that "ICANN plans to set up an oversight panel to take a firm stance against the alternative movement, claiming that there are 'solid technical grounds for a single authoritative root.'"). The report describes the arguments and explanations for the emergence of these rogue alternative roots. *See InterNIC, The Domain Name System: A Non-Technical Explanation—Why Universal Resolvability Is Important, at* https://www.internic.net/faqs/authoritative-dns.html (last visited Sept. 6, 2023).

22 Jon Postel, Domain Name System Structure and Delegation 1 (1994), *available at* https://datatracker.ietf.org/doc/html/rfc1591 (describing the domain name system). On the arguments on whether new gTLDs should be added, see ICANN, Report (Part One) of Working Group C (New Gtlds) Presented to Names Council (2000), *available at* http://www.icann.org/dnso/wgc-report-21mar00.htm; Supplemental Report to Names Council Concerning Working Group C (2000), *available at* https://archive.icann.org/en/dnso/wgc-supp-report-17apr00.htm;

exists. Listed under the ".edu" umbrella are Boston University and other educational institutions. No other Boston University can be listed. Under the name of each institution, other lower-level domain names can be listed and managed, such as "tfrankel." No other "tfrankel" can be listed.

There is a general belief that the inter-connectivity of the Internet depends on the integrity and maintenance of this hierarchical structure, and that unless the message senders and transferors comply with the same rules, or protocols, confusion will reign. Hence, like market standards of weights and measures and prohibitions on fraud, the Internet is governed by a structure of names, numbers and protocols.[23]

The intermediaries that form the Internet infrastructure are the ISPs, registries and registrars. ISPs receive and transfer messages usually to other ISPs and through them to the final destination.[24] Registries manage the database of the names under their umbrella in the pyramid. Thus, the "root registry" registers the ccTLDs and gTLDs.[25] Registries manage and publish the zone files of ccTLDs and gTLDs. Registrars manage names under specific gTLDs. The current uniform practice among the large ISPs is to follow the single root structure. Some people question the necessity of one root and maintain that dual roots will not necessarily disrupt the connectivity of the Internet.[26] But no one has made a serious attempt to experiment with two roots for fear of disrupting the smooth operation of the Internet.

ICANN, CONSIDERATION OF INTRODUCING NEW GENERIC TOP-LEVEL DOMAINS (2000), https://archive.icann.org/en/dnso/gtld-topic-20apr00.htm (all last visited Dec. 20, 2023).

23   To be sure, there are networks, and very large networks, that have different names, numbers and protocols. But if they are to interconnect with the global network, they must fit within the naming, numbering and protocols of the global Internet.

24   In addition, there are services that do not actually transfer the messages but facilitate the search for particular sites on the Internet, such as America Online.

25   DOMAIN NAME SERVICES ORGANIZATION, ROOT LEVEL REGISTRY RULES, THE MANNER OF ADDING NEW GTLDS TO THE INTERNET (1999), *formerly at* http://www.dnso.net/mhsc-tld.htm ("The function of the root registry is to register and advertise TLDs.").

26   *See* Kieren McCarthy, *The Insider's Guide to the ICANN Meeting,* REGISTER (Sept. 21, 2001), *at* https://theregister.co.uk/content/6/21533.html (last visited Sept. 6, 2023) (noting that "some within ICANN" have supported multiple roots).

2. The Power of Bestowing Internet Names and Numbers

An Internet "domain name" differs in value and function from a name in real space.[27] A domain name is the spark that breathes life and the very existence on the Internet. The loss of a name on the Internet is death without a trace. In fact, when reassigned, the name breathes life into another being. Our Internet names must be unique to us. More than in real space, the Internet name system deprives us of the freedom to use the names allocated to others. While in real space people with the same name can be distinguished by other means, on the Internet there is little distinguishing information about people. Names are the only means of recognition.[28] Therefore, name allocation and withdrawal can be a source of power and wealth.

Like the naming system, the management of the system is hierarchical, and so is the power to allocate names. Since all names derive from one source, that source reigns supreme, and like the vassals in the feudal system, each vassal source derives its power from the lord above it, until it reaches the pinnacle—the king. That king is ICANN.

3. Enter ICANN

ICANN was established to achieve a number of objectives. The foremost objective was to ensure the Internet stability and expand its capacity. ICANN was also required to increase the number of gTLDs and registries, to facilitate competition among them,[29] and to help establish a dispute settlement mechanism between holders of domain names and holders of registered

---

27 *See* Tamar Frankel, *The Common Law and Cyberspace* (2001), *at* https://papers.ssrn.com/sol3/papers.cfm?abstract_id=292614.

28 Because short names help memory, they are in short supply. Although we view the Internet as a source of new and more information, often the details are lost on Internet communications. For example, we can receive information quickly from all over the globe. But information about the senders and receivers is more limited than in face-to-face or even telephone interaction. As one dog in front of the computer says to another in a cartoon in THE NEW YORKER: "On the Internet, nobody knows you're a dog." Peter Steiner, THE NEW YORKER, July 5, 1993, *at* 61, 61.

29 *See ICANN Announces Decision on .com/.net/.org Domains,* COMPUTER & INTERNET LAW., June 2001, *at* 31 (describing the revised agreement between ICANN and the registry of ".com," ".org" and ".net," that VeriSign had acquired the registry and that Network Solutions, Inc. has been split, thus facilitating competition on the registry level); Sandra Dillich, *Network Solutions Loses .com, .net and .org,* COMPUTER DEALER NEWS, Feb. 25, 2000, *at* 42 (describing

trademarks.[30] The precise nature of ICANN's authority was not spelled out. Some viewed it as a forum for developing policy by building a consensus. Some viewed it as a far more proactive manager of a technology-based market, designed to monitor and evaluate the infrastructure actors of the naming and numbering system and its performance, as well as to prevent transgressions that endanger the system.

ICANN's lawmaking functions include allocation and regulation of some, though not all, lucrative infrastructure services, such as the registries and registrars,[31] and setting the qualifications of these actors.[32] ICANN can therefore create such businesses and limit entry into such businesses. Unlike governments, ICANN's mission is limited to its enterprise. The enterprise, however, affects many areas of human lives—business, culture, politics, community, public morals and private rights. Its reach is global. In that sense as well, ICANN is a lawmaker.

the negotiations that led to the agreement, and the history and summary of the agreement).

30 *See* ICANN Watch, *ICANN for Beginners, formerly at* http://www. icannwatch.org/icann4beginners.php; *now see* http://www.icannwatch. org/icann4beginners.shtml (last visited Dec. 22, 2023); Improvement of Technical Management of Internet Names and Addresses, 63 Fed. Reg. 8826 (Feb. 20, 1998) (*codified at* 15 C.F.R. ch. 13) (proposing a rule to improve the management of the Internet Domain Name System, and describing the infrastructure of the Internet). This rule was not passed. Instead, the DOC issued a Statement of Policy in the form of a White Paper, which stated the main objectives contained in the proposed rule. *See* Management of Internet Names and Addresses, 63 Fed. Reg. 31,741 (June 10, 1998).

31 *See* Sandra Dillich, *Network Solutions Loses .com, .net and .org,* Computer Dealer News, Feb. 25, 2000 (noting that registry services "became a huge revenue maker"). As to ISPs, aside from contracting with Regional Internet Registries for some policy-making intellectual property address block allocation, which involves little policy making, there are no qualifications or other regulation of ISPs.

32 *See* Saroja Ginshankar, *Internet Domain Name Registry Up for Bids,* InternetWeek, Feb. 15, 1999, LEXIS, News Library, News Group File. The monitoring and evaluation is to be determined by a committee of third parties. *See* ICANN, Preliminary Report, Meeting of the ICANN Board in Stockholm (2001), *at* https://www.icann.org/minutes/prelim-report-04jun01.htm (last visited Sept. 6, 2023) ("Whereas in resolution 01.60, the (ICANN) Board directed 'the President to prepare and present to the Board . . . a proposal to form a committee to recommend processes for monitoring the implementation of the new TLDs and evaluating the new TLD program, including any ongoing adjustments of agreements with operators or sponsors of new TLDs.'").

ICANN's structure is unique, and I may say, unwieldy. It consists of a board, a president and staff, and three "supporting organizations," the most problematic of which is the Domain Name Supporting Organization ("DNSO").[33] Each organization nominates three board members, while nine board members are elected by users. Elections by millions of people over the globe have not yet been achieved. ICANN's processes required transparency and public participation. This requirement has not been entirely met. Further, it is unclear whether ICANN was expected to establish policies or merely to approve policies established by its three supporting organizations. The DNSO did not succeed in reaching a consensus on proposed policies.[34] In its proposal to restructure ICANN, the staff has declared the current structure and constraints a failure, and proposed to simplify the structure.[35] Five directors representing the governments of each global region would substitute for the nine publicly elected directors. No review panel would be established to determine the board's policy authority. ICANN will move towards a corporate model of the traditional not-for-profit corporation vintage.

B. ICANN Emerged as a Weak Monopoly Because of the Circumstances Surrounding Its Creation

Two views explain the creation of ICANN. One view describes ICANN's creation as the expression of a consensus on a specific agenda among parties with different interests and views.[36] The

33   ICANN, *Domain Name Supporting Organization (DNSO), at* https://www.icann.org/dnso/dnso.htm (last visited Sept. 6, 2023). The DNSO structure does not contain a working group which deals with issues concerning the ccTLDs. For a chart of the ICANN organization, *see* ICANN Watch, *The ICANN-GAC Organization, at* https://www.icannwatch.org/archive/orgchart.gif (last visited Sept. 6, 2023) (ICANN organization chart by Tony Rutkowski).

34   *See infra* Part III.B.4. describing the disaffection of the ccTLD registries.

35   *See* ICANN, President's Report: ICANN–the Case for Reform (2002), *at* https://www.icann.org/general/lynn-reform-proposal-24feb02.htm (last visited Sept. 6, 2023).

36   In 1998, prior to ICANN's creation, the author chaired meetings entitled the International Forum on the White Paper. These meetings were held in Reston, Virginia, on July 1-2, 1998; Geneva, Switzerland, on July 24-25, 1998; Singapore, on August 11-13, 1998; and Buenos Aires, Argentina, on August 20-21, 1998. The author spoke to the group in Buenos Aires but did not chair that meeting. The participants represented many different stakeholders. The purpose of the meetings was to reach a rough consensus regarding the structure, governance and participation of the company that was to take over the management of the naming and numbering system of the Internet. The

other view on the creation of ICANN is also consensus-based.[37] But the consensus was about something else. The interested parties, such as the technical communities, the large business interests, Network Solutions, Inc. ("NSI") (that managed the root zone and the gTLDs ".com," ".net" and ".org"), the various governments, the large ISPs, the small ISPs and the small businesses that use the Internet, had very different views of what the Internet infrastructure should be and how it should be managed. Most importantly, they disagreed on who should have the power to manage the naming system. They were also very concerned about the possible "capture" of the naming and numbering system by one interest group. Therefore, their consensus on the issues was reached at a very high level of generality. The devil of the details was left to be resolved.

1. Power by Default: "I Will Not Claim Control if You Do Not Claim Control"[38]

A review of ICANN's creation and emerging power suggests that different interest groups agreed *not to claim control* if everyone else would not claim control of the naming and numbering system. ICANN's power was therefore created by default. No one interest group has agreed to put another interest group on the throne to manage and regulate the infrastructure of the Internet, and each group was anxious about capture by another.

There were many candidates for the job: (1) the United States and other governments; (2) the established technical communities headed by Dr. Jon Postel, who designed the system and managed it for over twenty years; (3) the large businesses; (4) the professionals who sought to participate in the infrastructure for profit; (5) people who claimed to represent the consumers or users; and (6) international communication organizations.

The United States, which triggered the emergence of the Internet, and the U.S. administration, which exercised the management power over the Internet naming and numbering system, did not seek to continue its hegemony. The administration was hard pressed by a number of countries to deAmericanize

---

consensus achieved in these meetings contributed to the establishment of ICANN. *See* Domain Name Handbook, *International Forum on the White Paper (IFWP), at* http://www.domainhandbook.com/ifwp.html (last visited Sept. 6, 2023).

37   *Id.*

38   *Id.*

the Internet. Other difficult political issues have arisen that the U.S. wished to avoid. For example, how to define a country entitled to a ccTLD, and how to convert into competition the monopoly position of registries, notably NSI (now VeriSign), that managed ".com," ".org" and ".net." The U.S. administration was not interested in mediating disputes between the business communities and the technical communities, since the solutions involved costs in dollars and time.

The U.S. administration was ready to offer the Internet to the world, but with strings attached. To de-Americanize the management and regulation of the Internet infrastructure without severing its American umbilical cord, the administration considered different avenues. Since the interested groups did not reach a consensus, the administration conducted meetings and produced a policy paper that seemed, at a high level, to represent a consensus not only between the U.S. groups, but also with foreign governments.[39]

While different governments demanded the deAmericanization of the Internet, none claimed to be the sole governor of the Internet infrastructure. It was recognized that none would succeed in realizing such a demand, and the only country which in fact controlled the infrastructure, namely the U.S., was unlikely to relinquish control to another country. Neither was the UN an acceptable alternative. Control over the Internet infrastructure required a nimble guiding management and sensitive rulemaking. The UN and its various organizations were considered too slow and inflexible to respond to the kaleidoscopic, fast-changing demands of the Internet.

The technical community, especially the Internet Assigned Numbers Authority ("IANA"), led by Dr. Postel, was a natural candidate for the management of the infrastructure of the Internet. It had been managing the infrastructure since the Internet's inception. Many members of the communities were in fact the ISPs and registries. They also commanded support of some European governments. These communities wanted to undertake the management and regulatory function. However, the U.S. business community and NSI did not agree to a transfer of control to the technical communities, and demanded a voice, even a decisive voice, in decisions concerning the Internet infrastructure. Therefore, a compromise between these two interest groups and

---

39   *Id.*

their different visions of the Internet had to be reached before a private corporation could be established.

The conflict between the technical communities and the business communities was complicated because many had members in each camp. Some "techies" were employed by large business organizations such as MCI (later WorldCom, Inc., then MCI Inc.), AT&T Corp. and IBM Corp. These persons were also involved in the Internet service providing activities. Thus, not all parts of the business communities necessarily objected to influence of the technical groups. On the other side of the coin were the registries, and especially NSI, that were publicly owned and operated as businesses rather than as volunteer or scientific enterprises. Thus, it would be more accurate to describe the conflict as a conflict between two philosophies and cultures. The one viewed the Internet as a tool for business development or as a source of profit from servicing. The other, rejecting the view of the Internet as a tool for "making money," viewed the Internet as the product of technological creativity, whose purpose was to continue to contribute to science, national society and the global community.[40]

The small business interests and those who claimed to represent the users and "net citizens" were not candidates for controlling the infrastructure, but demanded participation in the control.[41] They, too, were divided. Some aligned with technical communities and some with different clusters of interest, but many did not align with anyone.

It was recognized that technical decisions concerning the infrastructure could no longer be made by technology criteria alone. Political and business consequences of technical decisions mattered. The future body that would guide the infrastructure of the Internet had to consider all three criteria (technical, business and political), mediate among them and balance them correctly. This conclusion brought about the idea of an entirely new organization to meet the new demands.

The route to establishing the entity that would manage and regulate the Internet infrastructure had to be foggy. The U.S. administration wished to avoid "establishing" and "acquiring" a private corporation because such a corporation must be established

---

40   *Id.*

41   *Id.*

under an act of Congress.[42] There was concern that if the matter came before Congress it might become a problematic "political football." To avoid the required act, the administration had to avoid the "establishment" or "acquisition" of such a corporation. From the point of view of the administration and some members of Congress, the solution was to help create a private corporation, grounded in market principles, and an Internet infrastructure moved by competition. This creation would be an entity that no one established, but just came into being. In fact, that is the closest description of the emergence of ICANN. Not one invisible hand, but many invisible hands, brought it about. Had only one hand, as invisible as it might have been, propelled the entity into existence, other powerful hands would have been raised in protest. The flurry of negotiations, promises, some broken, some re-negotiated or abandoned, and alliances formed and reformed brought about an equilibrium that allowed the entity to emerge. The driving force of the negotiation and consensus seems to have been the recognition that no better alternative was available. ICANN was therefore born by default.[43]

2. ICANN's Initial Power Was Weak

In addition to ICANN's default creation, it was not very powerful either. The circumstances of its birth did not inspire much confidence or legitimacy. ICANN had no blessing of an authorizing statute.[44] It did not have the benefit of the invisible hand of the free market or the citizens' votes in a democratic regime. In fact,

---

42 Under federal law, the executive branch may establish and control a private sector corporation only under a statute. *See* Government Corporation Control Act of 1945, 31 U.S.C. §9102. *See also* A. Michael Froomkin, *Reinventing the Government Corporation,* 1995 U. ILL. L. REV. 543 (1995). Arguably, because the executive neither "established" nor "acquired" ICANN, the statute did not apply to it. ICANN has been operating on the basis of an agreement with the DOC. The DOC asserts its authority to enter into such agreements, but questions persist.

43 Congress was merely apprised of the emergence of ICANN. The ccTLD registries are currently paying ICANN a fee for services that they used to receive free from the U.S. government. It was suggested that they are willing to do so in order to "pry the Internet naming system from the U.S. government." *Revolt Threatens ICANN's Budget,* USA TODAY (Nov. 20, 2000), *formerly at* http://www.usatoday.com/life/cyber/tech/cti821.htm.

44 Under federal law, the executive branch may establish and control a private sector corporation only under a statute. *See* GCCA, 31 U.S.C. §9102. *See also* A. Michael Froomkin, *Wrong Turn in Cyberspace: Using ICANN to Route Around the APA and the Constitution,* 50 DUKE L.J. 17, 22-23 (2000).

it emerged as a result of negotiations among interest groups with the service of go-betweens. Its great leadership weakness was the image of secret negotiations, behind the scenes agreements, and mistrust of "outsiders." Mistrust breeds mistrust.

In addition, ICANN's mandate was general. Some of its missions posed conflicts between technological, business and political views. ICANN was required to establish additional gTLDs. But the largest corporations with the most famous brand names objected to any such addition because it imposed heavy costs on them in protecting their trademarks.[45] ICANN was required to create competition among registries, and especially to break up NSI's monopoly. Yet that monopoly was in part based on the infrastructure of the Interne t that required registries to maintain a central database to avoid duplications of the names and the numbers. In addition, the "ownership" or other form of entitlement of the names and the databases was not established. To create competition among registries and registrars required portability of the names, and demand for names coupled with the vision of a free market in the names gave the names the features of property with attendant unanticipated consequences, such as cybersquatting. Thus, ICANN's management decisions could have far-reaching consequences, and at the same time conflict with the desires of one or more of its supporting interest groups.

ICANN received the mantle of Dr. Postel as the manager of the naming and numbering system. But not quite. It did not have his authority nor the adoration of his followers, which had grown with twenty-five years of devoted service and good judgment. It did, however, have a contract with the DOC, but a conditional contract at that.[46] To become fully vested with the powers of the United States (whatever these are) over the systems, ICANN had

---

[45] A. Michael Froomkin, *Reinventing the Government Corporation,* 1995 U. Ill. L. Rev. 543, 547 (1995).

[46] Memorandum of Understanding Between the U.S. Department of Commerce and Internet Corporation for Assigned Names and Numbers (n.d.), *formerly at* http://www.icann.org/general/icann-mou-25nov98.htm, *now see* https://www.ntia.gov/page/memorandum-understanding-between-us-department-commerce-and-internet-corporation-assigned (last visited Dec. 22, 2023).

to meet additional conditions under a certain deadline.[47] These involved the heart of its control structure—public participation in its decision making and in its board. These conditions were precisely the ones that some of ICANN's promoters rejected. Elections are antithetical to self-perpetuating boards. Elections endanger the position of the existing controlling group and open the doors to capture of the institution.

In sum, when ICANN emerged, its mission and power were not clearly defined. Its strength lay in the lack of better alternatives. ICANN's power was strengthened at the outset by the highly reputable persons who populated its first board, and by a dedicated expert staff with significant knowledge of the Internet, its organizations and its history. This knowledge complemented the expertise of the board members. Needless to say, ICANN was not strong. The world sat back, folded its arms, and took a wait-and-see attitude. ICANN was not powerless, however. It was backed by a number of power centers: (1) the technical communities; (2) the large business communities, including the large ISPs; (3) NSI; and (4) the involved governments. This was ICANN's power base, and it was quite broad.[48]

III. Puzzle: How Does a Weak Monopoly Augment Its Power?

A. Consolidating the Power

1. Constitutional Documents: The Articles and Bylaws

ICANN's articles of incorporation and bylaws have the potential of providing the entity with significant power.[49] However, the entity's structure is also very complex, and the

---

47 ICANN did not meet the requirements of the DOC and was therefore not fully vested with the authority over the root. However, the DOC has averred its intention to make the transfer, and retreated from a clear intent. The question of ICANN's legal status was discussed in a General Accounting Office report of 2000. *See* Office of the Gen. Counsel, U.S. Gen. Accounting Office, Dep't of Commerce: Relationship With The Internet Corporation For Assigned Names and Numbers (2000), *formerly at* http://www.gao.gov/new.items/0g00033r.pdf.

48 This power base did not include recognized consumer representatives, except to the extent that national governments may be deemed to represent the interests of their citizens and residents.

49 *See ICANN,* Bylaws (2002), *formerly at* http://www.icann.org/general bylaws.htm; ICANN, Articles of Incorporation (1998), *available at* https://www.icann.org/general/articles.htm (last visited Sept. 6, 2023).

division of power among the different groups, such as the board on the one hand and the supporting organizations on the other hand, is not spelled out in the document. That is also because there was no clear consensus on the division of the power. Supporting organizations could designate their candidates to the board and could propose policies to the board. Although it seems to have been the consensus that the board could not reject the candidates, it was not clear whether the board had to accept the policy proposals and whether the board could initiate its own proposals. It was also not clear whether initiation would be limited to non-technical policies, and whether one could distinguish between technical, political and business considerations. Thus, the vagueness of the documents could provide ICANN with power, or rob it of power, depending on the implementation of its policies and solutions to the problems with which it would be presented.

2. The Contracts with Internet Service Providers and Registries

An important part of ICANN's power base is grounded in the contracts that ICANN negotiated with the Internet infrastructure operators, the registries and registrars. These contracts should rightly be added as part of ICANN's constitution. Said ICANN's President, Mike Roberts: "ICANN had to take the very informal handshake world of (Internet founder) Jon Postel and turn that into language that can be written down and form the basis of a legal arrangement."[50] ICANN sought to formalize its relationship with the government, the registries and the service providers through the mechanism of contracts.[51]

The contracts contain features that empower ICANN. For example, the parties to the contract are obligated to abide by ICANN's policies if these policies command consensus. A review board (to be established) has the authority to make a finding of the existence or absence of a consensus. The importance of these contracts cannot be exaggerated (because the definition of policy

50 Maureen Sirhal, *Net Governance: ICANN Makes Progress on Sticky Issue of Domains*, NAT'L J. TECH. DAILY, Feb. 6, 2001, LEXIS, News Library, News Group File. Such agreements have not yet materialized with most registries, let alone been standardized. *See* Maureen Sirhal, *Net Governance: European Domains Want ICANN's Attention*, NAT'L J. TECH. DAILY, Dec. 7, 2000, LEXIS, News Library, News Group File.

51 *See* Mark Sableman, *ICANN Faces Major Challenge with Country Codes*, NAT'L L.J., Dec. 18, 2000, *at* C10.

decision is vague). Thus, so long as ICANN's policy decisions command a consensus they are binding on the signatories of the contracts, that is, on the actors in the Internet infrastructure.[52]

Some economists have suggested the use of contracts as a response to the failures of the contestable markets theory, especially in the deregulation period. "The ultimate objective is to replace transitory regulation with the contracts that would have been in effect had they not been superseded by regulatory institutions."[53] Therefore, lawmakers should negotiate laws in the market, and pass laws that are as close as possible to the negotiated result had there been a market. The visible regulators' hand should be led by the visible hand of the parties. The contestable market theory and the use of contracts are proposed as alternatives to heavy-handed inefficient government regulation. ICANN is using contracts as a negotiated regulatory device.[54]

3. General Support for ICANN's Prime Directive: To Maintain the Stability of the Internet

ICANN's primary directive has had the support of many, if not all, powerful stakeholders. Both governments and businesses that invest millions in Internet commerce and in persuading their customers to use this new medium put a high premium on stability and operability of the Internet. Blackouts and other mishaps, even short lived, can cause heavy losses and terminate client relationships.

The prime directive of ICANN could be interpreted in different ways, some of which allow for more flexibility and experimentation than others. Many questions can be differently determined depending on this interpretation. For example, does stability require one root at all costs? Can a multitude of roots be designed in a way that would support stability and increased scope? Should experiments at the fringe of the Internet be encouraged, and if so, how can they be implemented once proven

---

52   In the proposed restructure of ICANN, the review board is eliminated. Conflict on whether a policy commands consensus is then likely to be determined among the parties, a court or other mechanism which the parties will establish at the time of dispute.

53   William B. Tye, THE THEORY OF CONTESTABLE MARKETS 121 (1990) (suggesting that contracts can be viewed as an extension of the Coase theorem).

54   *See* David Johnson & David Post, *And How Shall the Net Be Governed?: A Meditation on the Relative Virtues of Decentralized, Emergent Law, in* COORDINATING THE INTERNET 62 (Brian Kahin & James H. Keller eds., 1997).

not to endanger the stability? Should these experiments be left to the regulation of the market? If experiments are allowed, to what extent, if any, should enterprises that invested heavily in existing technology and structure have control over these experiments? Should these issues be raised now, or should they be raised when the existing structure is well established? Or, should they be raised when the experiments are launched, or when problems arise?

With respect to stability of the Internet, ICANN has taken a conservative attitude, in line with the interpretation of its stakeholders and many governments. It sought to standardize the Internet infrastructure. This interpretation strengthens ICANN's power. One root creates a natural monopoly that, by definition, vests decision and lawmaking power in the manager of the system. Any additional root weakens or completely undermines this power. So long as the main stakeholders view the prime directive as crucial to their own interests, ICANN must be endowed with sufficient power to implement this prime objective. That was and has remained a significant basis of ICANN's power.

4. Indirect Help from Congress

I believe that even though some members of Congress would have preferred to deal with Internet governance by legislation rather than mere monitoring, most members of the House of Representatives committees that dealt with the Internet were willing to take the "wait-and-see" attitude towards ICANN.[55] However, whether unwittingly or by design, Congress has also helped ICANN perform a task that seemed impossibly conflicted: creating additional gTLDs and facilitating greater competition among registries. The task met strong opposition from a large, important stakeholder constituency of ICANN: the owners of famous trademarks.[56] These stakeholders have been protecting their trademarks at great cost, and additional gTLDs could increase these costs because each new gTLD can breed trademark violations under its cap.

---

55   The doubts about the legality of ICANN persisted, and Congress requested the General Accounting Office to inquire how ICANN came into existence. *See* OFFICE OF THE GEN. COUNSEL, U.S. GEN. ACCOUNTING OFFICE, DEP'T OF COMMERCE: RELATIONSHIP WITH THE INTERNET CORPORATION FOR ASSIGNED NAMES AND NUMBERS 1 (2000), *formerly at* http://www.gao.gov/new.items/0g00033r.pdf.

56   *See* A. Michael Froomkin, *Wrong Turn in Cyberspace: Using ICANN to Route Around the APA and the Constitution*, 50 DUKE L.J. 17, 22-23 (2000).

Congress responded to the trademark owners in a way that reduced their objections to additional gTLDs. Congress passed a law to protect famous trademarks from dilution.[57] This was a fundamental change in trademark law, which was based on protection of consumers from confusion. In addition, ICANN established an option of less expensive resolution of disputes between trademark owners and domain name owners. The new statute and the less costly process by which trademark owners could protect their trademarks against competing domain names reduced the objection of the large corporations to the creation of new gTLDs.

In addition, congressional monitoring has helped ICANN by offering accurate information, criticism and a sense of the limits on ICANN's actions. For example, when ICANN proposed to levy a $1 charge on all registrars world-wide for every domain name registration, the protest, which was aired also in Congress, caused ICANN to back off.[58] Some would consider this a failure. I consider this event a success. Congress helps ICANN evaluate its trial and error attempts at expanding its power.

5. Help From the Courts

A recent decision regarding a domain name indirectly supports ICANN's power.[59] This case involves a claim by a national government. The government of South Africa sued an American enterprise that used the words "South Africa" in its domain names.[60] The government of South Africa maintained that the name is its property.[61] The District Court for the Southern District of New York denied jurisdiction and referred the parties to arbitration in accordance with ICANN's procedures.[62] The decision indirectly supports ICANN's power. Courts are unlikely to entertain claims of sovereign powers to ccTLDs, and the issue is designed to be resolved in accordance with the process established

---

57　Consolidated Appropriations Act of 2000, Pub. L. No. 106-113, §§3001-3010, 113 Stat. 1501, 1501A-521 to -552 (1999) (codified in scattered sections of 15, 16 & 28 U.S.C.).

58　*See* Mark Sableman, *ICANN Faces Major Challenge with Country Codes,* Nat'l L.J., Dec. 18, 2000.

59　*See Virtual Countries, Inc. v. Republic of South Africa*, 148 F. Supp. 2d 256 (S.D.N.Y. 2001), *aff'd*, 300 F.3d 230 (2d Cir. 2002).

60　*Id.* at 259.

61　*Id.*

62　*Id.* at 268.

by ICANN. It is unlikely that any and all uses of a state's name will be barred by the arbitration tribunal. Thus, ICANN will be freed of making difficult decisions. It seems that the government of South Africa and some other governments have determined to protect their names by internal legislation.[63] This approach as well relieves ICANN from the burden of determining the issue and exposing a weakness if it cannot implement its decision.

6. Mediation and Negotiations with and Among Stakeholders

ICANN has chosen appropriate methods for consolidating power. Before decisions were made public, the governments and other large stakeholders were consulted and a consensus was obtained. Only then would the results be published. Further, ICANN has not always insisted on exerting authority. It deals with powerful constituencies by negotiation rather than ruling. However, every agreement with any such constituency helps build precedents for agreements with others, thereby helping to establish future customary rules. Moreover, when a conflict arose among powerful stakeholders, ICANN was often inclined to play the role of a mediator rather than an arbitrator. It has provided an effective forum for negotiation and a face-saving intermediary service. That increased its value to those participants. Repeat requests to ICANN augmented its power.

However, consensus-building negotiations make it harder to gain public support and broad leadership. The process is far from public and the method limits ICANN's freedom to factor in public comments. Therefore, the solicitation of public comments and input seems to be a sham. To some extent it is. That may explain why ICANN's power rests primarily on its constituencies and far less on public support and leadership.

B. Demonstrating ICANN's Rising Power

Recent events concerning ccTLDs demonstrate that ICANN's power is on the rise. ICANN's interaction with ccTLD registries has increased in recent years. The context and substance of these interactions differ, but all indicate the nature and level of ICANN's power.

---

63 *See Bill on Internet Due Soon,* AFRICA NEWS, Oct. 4, 2001, LEXIS, News Library, News Group File; *Cyber Cops to Ensure Safe Surfing,* AFRICA NEWS, Mar. 22, 2002, LEXIS, News Library, News Group File (noting that the bill was tabled in March 2002).

1. Country Code Top–Level Domain Names

ccTLDs are two-letter names designed to inform about the physical location of name holders. They are on the same level as gTLDs. With the rise of the value of gTLDs, such as ".com," the value of ccTLDs has risen as well. That is because under a ccTLD, one can create many new (and sometimes known) gTLDs under its umbrella. ccTLDs are similar to TLDs except that they are limited to existing political real entities (countries), regardless of how we define them.[64]

When the value and importance of names and their management was not accompanied by political or economic values, ccTLDs and their registries—delegates of the power to manage the database of the domain names under their authority—were recognized generously.[65] For example, IANA, which preceded ICANN, recognized the delegation of a ccTLD to Palestine, and thereafter confirmed a reassignment of the delegation to other registries.[66]

The use of ccTLDs varies. In some countries, they are used as gTLDs that have a similar name as the country's name. In other countries, they represent a political geography.[67] Some countries

---

64   The argument of whether a country can assert exclusive right to its name was raised in a United States court. *See Virtual Countries, Inc. v. Republic of South Africa*, 148 F. Supp. 2d 256 (S.D.N.Y. 2001), *aff'd*, 300 F.3d 230 (2d Cir. 2002). The district court did not assert jurisdiction and suggested that the parties resort to the international arbitration system provided for disputes concerning domain names. *Id.* at 268.

65   *See* John C. Klensin, Internet Engineering Task Force, Reflections on the DNS, RFC 1591, and Categories of Domains (2000), *formerly at* http://public.research. mimesweeper.com/standards/IETF/Draft/draft-klensin-1591-reflections-02. txt (describing ccTLDs and gTLDs and the controversies involving their delegation).

66   To avoid making a political decision, IANA followed a list by ISO 3166 Maintenance Agency, and agreed to the re-delegation of Palestine when Palestine was accorded the status of "Occupied Palestine Territory." IANA, Iana Report on Request For Delegation of the .ps Top Level Domain (2000), *at* https:// www.icann.org/general/ps-report-22mar00.htm (last visited Sept. 6, 2023) (containing IANA's report and analysis which led to the recommendation to approve the re-delegation). *See also* International Organization for Standardization, *ISO 3166 Maintenance Agency (ISO 3166/MA)*, *formerly at* http://www.din.de/gremien/nas/nabd/iso3166ma (describing the complete list of country names and ISO 3166-1 Alpha-2 code elements—the ISO country code used on the Internet).

67   *See* Jon Postel, Domain Name System Structure and Delegation 1 (1994), *formerly at* ftp://ftp.isi.edu/in-notes/rfc1591.txt. Part of this description has changed with the years. The principles, however, remained the same. *See*

have privatized (sold) their ccTLDs, as the U.S. government is considering doing.[68] Other countries deem the registries of ccTLDs to be the delegates of the governments and under their control.

2. The Dispute over ccTLD ".au" Between the Registry and the Australian Government

In 1986, Professor Robert Elz received from Dr. Postel the delegated authority over the registry of Australia's ccTLD—".au." Even though the registry had the power to create second-level domains, such as ".com.au" and ".net.au,"[69] Professor Elz seemed to believe that the main Internet services should not be commercial.[70] No commercial use also meant no value for the names. Consequently, "Australia has never had a cybersquatting problem like the United States has."[71] No one compiles names for sale.

The government of Australia, however, has different priorities, planning a far more aggressive commercial development of the

ICANN, ICP-1: INTERNET DOMAIN NAME SYSTEM STRUCTURE AND DELEGATION (1999), *at* https://www.icann.org/icp/icp-1.htm (last visited Sept. 6, 2023) (describing ICANN's administration practices, and noting that IANA has remained the overall authority for day-to-day administration of the naming system, intellectual property addresses, autonomous system numbers and TLDs, and other aspects of the system). The document includes the source where the "procedures to be followed in requesting TLD delegations or changes" can be found. *Id.* The document contains the qualification requirements for TLD managers. *Id.*

68   *See* NAT'L TELECOMMS. AND INFO. ADMIN., THE DIGITAL OPPORTUNITY TRUST: THE DOT IN .US, *at* https://www.ntia.doc.gov/ntiahome/domainname/usrfc2/comments.html (last visited Sept. 6, 2023) (proposing an elaborate plan to manage ".us" for the benefit of all U.S. citizens); *Commerce Department Poised to Accept Bids for .us*, NAT'L. J. TECH. DAILY, June 1, 2001, LEXIS, News Library, News Group File. *See also* ICANN Watch, *More on the .us Solicitation, formerly at* http://www.icannwatch.org/article.php?sid=208 (June 14, 2001).

69   *See* Kate Mackenzie, *Domains Taken from Elz*, AUSTRALIAN, Feb. 5, 2002, *at* 29; *Multimedia Seeks .au Registry*, AUSTRALIAN FIN. REV., Dec. 3, 2001, *at* 42 (Professor Elz assigned the ".au" rights to a "commercial spin-off" of Melbourne University–Melbourne IT).

70   It seems that Professor Elz controlled more than the database containing the current domain name holders. See Kirsty Needham, *Australian Government to Take Over Domain Names*, SYDNEY MORNING HERALD, Jan. 22, 2001, at 35 (noting that the government agency bought a database of all domain names registered in Australia).

71   Kirsty Needham, *Internet's Reclusive Pioneer Hangs on to Keys to Web*, SYDNEY MORNING HERALD, June 13, 2001, *at* 25, *formerly at* http://old.smh.com.au/news/0106/13/biztech/biztech3.html.

Internet,[72] as well as tighter government control over domestic Internet use. [73] It established the authority "auDA,"[74] and required Professor Elz to re-delegate the registry's functions to this authority. The re-delegation of the ".au" space would also affect the sub-domains.[75] Professor Elz agreed to redelegate, but it appeared unlikely that he would do so until certain conditions had been met. [76] A year later, the redelegation had still not taken place.[77] On June 13, 2001, a news headline stated: *Internet's Reclusive Pioneer Hangs on to Keys to Web.*[78] Interestingly, Professor Elz was deemed *not to have responded* to the government's request—"just not doing anything"—rather than *refused the request.*[79] The government viewed this distinction as "relatively important."[80] In September 2001, ICANN announced that it had awarded control of the ".au"

---

72   National Office for the Information Economy, *Reforming .au Domain Name Administration,* formerly at http://www.noie.gov.au/projects/information%5Feconomy/domains%5Fau/index.htm (The website notes that government recognition of "effective administration of the .au domain space" is "important to the development of e-commerce in Australia.").

73   *See* ICANN Watch, *AUDA Seeks ICANN's Help to Force .au Redelegation,* formerly at http://www.icannwatch.org/article.php?sid=197 (June 6, 2001) (the Australian authority suggests that Professor Elz's administration had been slow, but did not allege any wrongdoing).

74   James Riley, *New Board Set Up for Domain Rule,* Australian, Apr. 27, 1999, at 49, 49.

75   *See Push for Name Controls,* Age (Melbourne), Mar. 7, 2000, at 1 ("The policy and administration of the .au domain would affect the sub-domains.").

76   *Dot .au Domain Name Registration Gets Nasty,* Bus. Rev. Weekly (Australia), May 19, 2000, at 44 (the article states that it was "unlikely Elz (would) relinquish his authority until auDA [had] secured the confidence of the industry and [was] endorsed by the National Office for the Information Economy.").

77   For a precedent by which IANA redelegated a ccTLD of an island of forty-nine residents, with the support of all but two of its adult inhabitants, *see* Jeri Clausing, *Pacific Islands Seek Control of Internet Designations,* N.Y. Times, Feb. 14, 2000, at C1. *See also* Mark Sableman, *ICANN Faces Major Challenge with Country Codes,* Nat'l L.J., Dec. 18, 2000, at C10.

78   Kirsty Needham, *Internet's Reclusive Pioneer Hangs on to Keys to Web,* Sydney Morning Herald, June 13, 2001, at 25, *formerly at* http://old.smh.com.au/news/0106/13/biztech/biztech3.html ("(Professor Elz) refused to relinquish his historic guardianship, flatly ignoring requests from the Federal Government to pass control of the country's Internet addressing system to a new regulatory body. The clash is one of the last stand-offs between the old school of the Internet and the commercial interests that now dominate it.").

79   *Id.*

80   Kate Mackenzie, *Tough Call on Names for ICANN,* Australian, June 26, 2001, at 33, 33.

domain to auDA.[81] However, Elz refused to release the ".org.au" and ".id.au" second-level domains, and they were seized from him in February 2002.[82]

The power relationship between a sovereign country, the registry of its name and ICANN is unclear. ICANN and IANA published the relevant information in 1999,[83] yet the power relationship is being established by actions rather than by words and rules. Arguably, a country should be entitled to its own name. But if the name has been assigned by a private body and used by a private individual, then presumably it cannot be the property of a government.[84] The entitlement to the names is a subject worthy of a separate paper.[85] The important and interesting point for the purpose of this Article is the fact that the government of Australia approached ICANN for help.[86] After all, Professor Elz was an Australian resident and perhaps an Australian citizen. The government could have introduced a bill that would have required the redelegation. It perhaps could have imposed a fine by law or used eminent domain over the ccTLD to requisition the name

---

81 *See* Kevin Murphy, *ICANN Hands .au Domain to Aussie Non-Profit*, COMPUTER WIRE, Sept. 5, 2001, LEXIS, News Library, News Group File.

82 *See* Kate Mackenzie, *Domains Taken from Elz*, AUSTRALIAN, Feb. 5, 2002, *at* 29.

83 ICANN, ICP-1: INTERNET DOMAIN NAME SYSTEM STRUCTURE AND DELEGATION (1999), *at* https://www.icann.org/icp/icp-1.htm (last visited Sept. 6, 2023). On transfer and disputes over delegation of TLDs, IANA should receive communications from both parties. It takes no action until the parties agree, noting that "it is far better when the parties can reach an agreement" because of the time it would otherwise take and that "it is appropriate for interested parties to have a voice in the selection of the designated manager." *Id.*

84 *See* Kate Mackenzie, *Domain Standoff Tests ICANN*, AUSTRALIAN IT (June 21, 2001).

85 *See id.* (suggesting that sovereign countries should have control over their names and over the registries, but if the names are used as gTLDs, with the consent of the governments, the names should be treated as such).

86 *See* Kirsty Needham, *Internet's Reclusive Pioneer Hangs on to Keys to Web*, SYDNEY MORNING HERALD, June 13, 2001, *formerly at* http://old.smh.com.au/news/0106/13/biztech/biztech3.html. (The representative of the government "has written to the Internet's governing body, the International (sic) Corporation for Assigned Names and Numbers, requesting his organisation be recognised as the peak Internet body in Australia, not Mr Elz."); Kate Mackenzie, *Domain Standoff Tests ICANN*, AUSTRALIAN IT (June 21, 2001) (noting that such an application is "virtually unprecedented" in that the delegate is refusing the redelegation and that the other application for redelegation involved Pitcairn Island).

and appoint its own delegate. It took none of these steps. Instead, it sought ICANN's intervention in the matter.[87] Other countries have taken another route. They have asserted their power over the management of their ccTLD, and passed laws to give the assertion real teeth.[88] These steps, however, do not weaken ICANN, though they do not strengthen it either.

3. The Rebellion of the ccTLD Registries

The registries of ccTLDs relate in various ways to the governments of the countries to which they provide access, and these differences are reflected in relationships between the ccTLD registries and ICANN. A number of small countries have allowed registries, for a fee, to use their ccTLDs for commercial purposes, like gTLDs.[89] These registries act and relate to the system and to ICANN as registries of gTLDs do. They have signed contracts with

---

87   See ICANN Watch, *AUDA Seeks ICANN's Help to Force .au Redelegation,* *formerly at* http://www.icannwatch.org/article.php?sid=197 (June 6, 2001) (administrators of ccTLDs who have not been "designated managers" in the database of IANA have sought ICANN's redelegation but were denied the request, except for Canada). What would prevent the government of the Ukraine from taking such steps if the registry were stationed in the Ukraine? *See* Julia Barton, *Ukraine's Domain in Dot-Dispute,* WIRED NEWS (June 22, 2001), *formerly at* http://www.wired.com/news/politics/0,1283,44012,00.html. See also George Kirikos, Red Alert: ICANN and Verisign Proposal Would Allow Any Government in the World to Seize Domain Names, *in* https://freespeech.com/2023/04/19/red-alert-icann-and-verisign-proposal-would-allow-any-government-in-the-world-to-seize-domain-names/ (April 19, 2023).

88   Early in March 2002, the South African government proposed legislation, the Electronic Communications and Transactions Bill, which would nationalize the administration of its ccTLD ".za." If enacted, the law would prohibit any organization from continuing its operation as a ".za" administrator. *See Bill on Internet Due Soon,* AFRICA NEWS, Oct. 4, 2001, LEXIS, News Library, News Group File; *Cyber Cops to Ensure Safe Surfing,* AFRICA NEWS, Mar. 22, 2002, LEXIS, News Library, News Group File (noting that the bill was tabled in March 2002). The government of Ireland has also taken steps to assert its jurisdiction over the administration of its ccTLD. *See* Denis Kelleher, *Cybersquatters' Rights Go West Under New Laws,* IRISH TIMES, May 15, 2000, *at* 8 (noting that legislation would allow the Minister of Public Enterprise to control rules governing domain name registration in Ireland); Karlin Lillington, *Digital Gesture by President Makes History,* IRISH TIMES, July 11, 2000, *at* 16 (noting passage of legislation).

89   *See, e.g.,* IANA, IANA REPORT ON REQUEST FOR REDELEGATION OF THE .PN TOP-LEVEL DOMAIN (2000), *available at* https://www.icann.org/general/pn-report-11feb00.htm (last visited Sept. 6, 2023) (Pitcairn Island); ICANN Watch, *VeriSign Buzzes with the .bz Biz(ness), formerly at* http://www.icannwatch.org/article.php?sid=185 (May 31, 2001); .NU, .NU Domain /IUS-N Mission, *formerly at* http://www.nunames.nu/ about/about.cfm (last visited Apr. 20, 2002); The

ICANN as required, and pay registration fees. But these registries are a minuscule minority of the 240 ccTLD registries. The others, such as those serving France, Germany and the U.K., are generally the designates of the governments of those countries, and the governments assert the right to re-delegate the management of the ccTLDs to others. Generally, as between the registries and the governments this is not an issue, and the registries consider themselves as an arm of their governments to further their governments' political and social policies.

Although these registries have been paying ICANN dues that cover about a third of ICANN's budget, many have not signed ICANN's contracts. Because they are not uniform in their functions and relationships to their governments, and because ICANN does not service all registries, a standard contract does not fit all of them. The text of these contracts has been negotiated for some time, and a number of contract models have been developed both for those registries that ICANN services and those that it does not.[90] In the process, feathers have been ruffled. In one case, ICANN has written to their governments, and this letter has raised the ire of the registries because some have interpreted the language to invite a review of the registries' performance.[91] In

---

.tv Corporation, *About Us, formerly at* http://www.tv/en-def-e9763cedc23f/en/about/about_company_overview.shtml?Hhtype=content6/20/01.

90   For a draft of a contract between ICANN and ccTLD registries, see ICANN, *CENTR Draft Contract for Services, formerly at* http://www.icann.org/ cctlds/centr-7th-draft-contract-20sep00.htm. For a draft of a proposed unsponsored TLD agreement with ICANN, dated September 21, 2001, *see* ICANN, *Proposed Unsponsored TLD Agreement, at* https://www.icann.org/tlds/agreements/unsponsored/registry-agmt-26apr01.htm (Apr. 26, 2001) (last visited Sept. 6, 2023). For a discussion draft of a ccTLD Manager-ICANN "Status Quo" Agreement, *see* ICANN, *Discussion Draft of ccTLD ManagerICANN "Status-Quo" Agreement, at* https://www.icann.org/yokohama/draft-cctld-status-quo-agreement-05jul00.htm (July 5, 2000) (last visited Sept. 6, 2023); William New, *Net Governance: ICANN Nears Deal on Country-Specific Domains,* Nat'l J. Tech. Daily, Mar. 12, 2001, LEXIS, News Library, News Group File. *See also Revolt Threatens ICANN's Budget,* USA Today (Nov. 20, 2000), *formerly at* http://www.usatoday.com/life/cyber/tech/cti821.htm.

91   *See* ICANN, *Discussion Draft of Letter to Governments Regarding ccTLD Managers, at* https://www.icann.org/cctlds/draft-letter-to-govts-12nov00.htm (Nov. 12, 2000) (last visited Sept. 6, 2023); Mark Ward, *Name Row Threatens the Net,* BBC News (Nov. 28, 2000), *formerly at* http://news.bbc.co.uk/hi/english/sci/tech/newsid_1043000/1043509.stm.

sum, ICANN's relationship with many of these registries has not yet been formalized, and the task is formidable.[92]

Historically, both ICANN and the ccTLD registries have adopted a "hands off" approach towards each other's activities. That has changed as ICANN sought to formalize its relationship with these registries—establishing controlling measures over them—and the registries demanded a greater role in ICANN and its policy decision making.[93] This is significant. The registries did not repudiate or question ICANN's authority. On the contrary, they demanded a greater voice in its power structure, that is, they demanded membership on its board.[94] The latest proposed structure of ICANN might resolve the issue. ccTLDs or their governments will pay dues to ICANN. The governments will occupy a board seat, however, and that might satisfy the demand for a greater voice in ICANN's government. ICANN's power as an entity will then be augmented by further support and money.

4. The Three Events Demonstrate ICANN's Increasing Power

The three events described above differ. One involves a dispute between a sovereign state and a registry of its ccTLD. The second is a dispute is between ccTLD registries, the DNSO and ICANN. The third case represents a disagreement between ICANN

---

92   *See* Maureen Sirhal, *Net Governance: ICANN Makes Progress on Sticky Issue of Domains,* Nat'l J. Tech. Daily, Feb. 6, 2001, LEXIS, News Library, News Group File; Mark Sableman, *ICANN Faces Major Challenge with Country Codes,* Nat'l L.J., Dec. 18, 2000.

93   Juliana Gruenwald, *Domain Group Revolts Against ICANN, formerly at* http://www.zdnet.com/zdnn/stories/news/0,4586,2767690.html (May 31, 2001); Andrew Orlowski, *Country Domain Chiefs Prefer Jaw-Jaw to War-War,* Register (June 14, 2001), *formerly at* http://www.theregister.co.uk/ content/6/19712.html.

94   ICANN's relationship to the registry of ".us" is unclear, as is the fate of the ccTLD. It is likely, however, that whoever wins the bid on this ccTLD will have to conform to ICANN's policies. *See* ICANN Watch, *More on the .us Solicitation, formerly at* http://www.icannwatch.org/article.php?sid=208 (last visited Apr. 21, 2002). *But see* Brian Kahin, *Making Policy by Solicitation: The Outsourcing of .us, at* http://icannwatch.org/essays/kahin.htm (July 16, 2001) (last visited Sept. 6, 2023) (suggesting that the winning contractor will determine policies and criticizing the current proposal to auction ".us"). While prior to 1999, IANA determined policy and NSI acted as a registry and performed the registration, after 1999, the policy function shifted to ICANN. NSI continued as a registry and registration became competitive, supervised by ICANN. It seems that under this plan, if ICANN is not the supervisor of the contract operator, it would be losing some of its hegemony.

and an aspiring ccTLD registry. All three events demonstrate recognition of ICANN's power to determine the existence and nature of ccTLDs, and the power to affect, at least by qualifications and imposition of fees, the identity and functions of the registries of these ccTLDs. The Australian government applied to ICANN to determine its dispute with the existing registry of its ccTLD.[95] Professor Elz may have implied ICANN's power to select or qualify registries because indirectly he based his rights on Dr. Postel's appointment rather than on the appointment by his government. The ccTLD registries felt that the DNSO, to which these registries belonged, did not represent the registries' interests. Therefore, the registries left the DNSO, but did not leave ICANN. Instead they demanded a more prominent place in its organization: a separate supporting organization and the right to appoint, select or recommend directors to its board.[96] The registries were critical of ICANN's operating practices but not of ICANN "as an organization."[97] The registries argued that there should be "no taxation without representation."[98] The use of these words is revealing. The power to tax is governmental; the right to representation is that of the citizen. It is unclear, however, whether the registries placed themselves in the position of citizens and ICANN—in the position of a government. That is because the

---

95   *See* ICANN Watch, *AUDA Seeks ICANN's Help to Force .au Redelegation,* *formerly at* http://www.icannwatch.org/article.php?sid=197 (June 6, 2001).

96   *See* Laura Rohde, *Defections at ICANN's Support Organization,* INDUSTRY STANDARD.COM, June 4, 2001, LEXIS, News Library, News Group File; Maureen Sirhal, *Net Governance: European Domains Want ICANN's Attention,* NAT'L J. TECH. DAILY, Dec. 7, 2000, LEXIS, News Library, News Group File. For the language of the registries' resolution, *see* WorldWide Alliance of Top Level Domain Names, *Executive Summary of ccTLD Stockholm Meeting on 31 May and 1 June 2001,* *formerly at* http://www.wwtld.org/meetings/cctld/Stockholm2001/Executive_ summary_.01June2001.html. Arguably, not all registries were of the same mind. Of the over 250 registries, only thirty-one voted to make the demand and take the action. However, the others did not object nor abstain, but simply did not take part in the process. *See* Mark Ward, *Name Row Threatens the Net,* BBC NEWS (Nov. 28, 2000), *formerly at* http://news.bbc.co.uk/hi/english/ sci/ tech/newsid_1043000/1043509.stm.

97   *See* Laura Rohde, *Defections at ICANN's Support Organization,* INDUSTRY STANDARD.COM, June 4, 2001, LEXIS, News Library, News Group File.

98   *Id. See also* Mark Ward, *Net Groups in World Wide Wrangle,* BBC NEWS (July 4, 2000), *at* http://news.bbc.co.uk/hi/english/sci/tech/newsid_817000/817657. stm (last visited Sept. 6, 2023) (stating that the registries believe that the costs levied on them stem from legal costs of ICANN's dealing with NSI, and refuse to pay for costs over which they had no control).

registries viewed their payments as fees for specific services and not as financing the operations of ICANN generally. But perhaps they only meant that if they financed ICANN's operations they ought to have a say about the way the money is spent. In any event, the registries recognized ICANN as the regulator of the ccTLDs, both by explicitly mentioning their recognition and by demanding greater power in the organization.

5. The Position of the U.S. Department of Commerce

On June 25, 2001, the DOC responded to a request by Mr. William H. Bode on behalf of Atlantic Root Network, Inc. ("Atlantic"). Atlantic was concerned about ICANN's process in selecting new TLDs. The DOC stated in part:

> In July 1998, the Department of Commerce made it clear that it would not participate in the selection process of new TLDs as set forth in the Statement of Policy, entitled Management of Internet Names and Addresses. . . . In the Statement of Policy, the Department recognized that the selection of new TLDs should be conducted by the private sector through a not-for-profit organization, globally representative of the Internet stakeholder community. The Department recognized ICANN as that organization in November 1998 through a Memorandum of Understanding.

> We note that at its May 2001 board of directors meeting, ICANN approved the establishment of a New TLD Evaluation Process Planning Task Force (Task Force) ro (sic) monitor the implementation process and to evaluate the selection process of the new TLDs. The ICANN board resolution stated that the Task Force will make recommendations to the ICANN board and the Internet community regarding the selection process. It is our understanding that the Task Force will allow public input when formulating its recommendations. We encourage you to participate in this opportunity. In a recent letter to ICANN, the Department encouraged ICANN to move forward in the selection of new TLDs in order to increase competition in the domain name space.

> Again, we encourage you to direct Atlantic Root Network's concern regarding ICANN's selection process directly to ICANN.

Sincerely,
(Signed) John F. Sopko
Acting Assistant Secretary for Communications
and Information[99]

The letter speaks for itself, making it clear that the U.S. supports ICANN in this matter, and recognizes ICANN's power most explicitly. The government encouraged the complainant to apply to ICANN. It is not surprising that the only party that did not concede ICANN's power was the aspiring rejected registry.

6. The Latest Move to Restructure

The latest move of ICANN's staff to restructure demonstrates how the institution is reaching for power. The proposal would greatly minimize constraints over the board and the staff. It would eliminate nine publicly elected directors and substitute for them fewer—(five)—representatives of governments reflecting the five regions of the globe.[100] Thus, each of ICANN's board members will represent specific identified interests, and will be selected by these interests. Governments will presumably ensure that ICANN will be better endowed and staffed. If this proposal is put into effect and if it works, ICANN will become stronger. At the same time, if its members contain each other's claims to hegemony, its overall powers may remain in check.

IV. BOUNDARIES OF POWER

A. Contestable Markets Theory

The introduction to this Article describes the theory of contestable markets. ICANN's circumstances (from its first birthday to its third birthday) bring to mind this theory and help explain ICANN's evolution. In fact, the inadequacies of the theory in the markets context are less pronounced in the context of power. I assume that the stability of the Internet requires the existence of a single root. I further assume that if more than one

---

99   Letter from John F. Sopko, Acting Assistant Secretary for Communications and Information, U.S. Department of Commerce, to William H. Bode, Partner, Bode & Beckman, LLP (June 25, 2001), *quoted in* ICANN Watch, *Commerce Dept: We Don't Do TLDs, formerly at* http://www.icannwatch.org/article.php?sid=237&mode=nested&order=0 (July 8, 2001).

100 *See* ICANN, PRESIDENT'S REPORT: ICANN–THE CASE FOR REFORM (2002), *at* https://www.icann.org/general/lynn-reform-proposal-24feb02.htm   (last visited Sept. 6, 2023).

manager manages the root, the financial and social costs of the Internet would rise. The two cooks will spoil the broth. Therefore, the structure of the Internet naming and numbering system mandates a single manager—a natural monopolist. I assume further that there is no superpower that regulates ICANN. The question is whether this monopoly will result in an excessive exercise of power, similar to excessive charges that a monopolist would extort from consumers.

B. The Nature of the Market for Power

The market that is discussed here is the *market for managing the numbering and naming system.* While in the business market competitors seek rents represented mostly by money, the rents from the power of ICANN are varied. These rents include the ability of the power holder to ensure the stability of the Internet and the integrity of the naming and numbering system. The power holder can guard over the technical integrity of the system, or maintain and expand the value of its investments in the current system as registry or ISP. The power holder can control the system for political reasons or protect one's trademarks by freezing or reducing the number of additional upper-level domain names.

Potential competitors may be interested in social benefits, and the stronger they are as potential competitors, the greater is ICANN's constraint on its power to conflict with these social benefits. These self-interested goals cannot be achieved unilaterally because the Internet is dependent on the support and actions of many others with other agendas (e.g., governments, legislatures and different ISPs). They must all agree to the management's edicts. By their consent to ICANN they can achieve their own self-interested objectives, at least to an acceptable degree.[101] It is

101 ICANN's power and the power of money are similar. Both are a store of value through which other objectives can be achieved. In fact, these are two different aspects of freedom and coercion. It is important to note that the *purpose* for which power is held is not the topic here. Power, like money, can be obtained voluntarily by consent from others, and usually in an exchange. Power, like money, can also be obtained from others by violence and extortion. The use of money, however, is generally more limited than the use of power. Money can be used coercively if it is necessary to obtain values (as sets) which other persons want. The person who has bread and would not part with it except through money has power over the hungry person. Yet this power is based on the possession of the bread, not the money.

the management power and its law-making capabilities that are the product in this market.[102]

The power for which there is a market in this case is of two kinds. One relates to particular actions in the exercise of management and lawmaking—"specific power." The other is the power to take over all the managerial and lawmaking activities— "general power." Firms that produce a number of related products can "cross-subsidize" their products and thereby block market entry to competitors that produce only one type of product. Arguably, like business corporations, ICANN can cross-subsidize one type of special power by another type of special power. For example, it can subsidize qualification requirements for other less stringent contract terms. However, many of ICANN's potential competitors, such as governments, are also multi-product firms in this sense. They too can subsidize one special power by another. The difference between these potential competitors and ICANN is in their institutional structure. As compared to ICANN, they have limited powers outside their territories but greater power within their territories. Even ISPs have some multi-product capabilities and can cross-subsidize. Thus, ICANN's competitors seem to be stronger than one-product business competitors.

C. The Competitors that Present a Constraining Force to the Monopolist

Under the contestable markets theory, competitors who can constrain the monopolist are those whose sunken costs are similar to the monopolist's sunken costs. Sunken costs for a general power are the costs of establishing a broad supporting coalition to take over ICANN's general power or at least to create a credible threat of such a possible takeover. Thus, if the members of ICANN's current supporting coalition were dissatisfied with the existing ICANN and had sufficient power to establish a different entity, they would present a formidable threat to ICANN's existence, and could force it to restructure or comply in other ways.

---

102 ICANN's power can be analogized to the power of other managers and the market for chief executive officers. They compete for the position of managers by obtaining the consent (or at least the passive non-intervention) of shareholders, nominators, existing top management, unions and perhaps others that wield power in the corporation. Or they may only receive the support of the nominators. They do, however, have competitors. Their market is small, though not a monopoly. But it may be sufficiently small to resemble a contestable market.

Alternatively, if a coalition of other competitors is sufficiently strong to convince the actors in the Internet infrastructure to cease following ICANN's instruction and the single root, the possibility and existence of such a coalition would deter ICANN from exercising any power in a way that would displease this coalition. In February 2002, I believed that this scenario is unlikely. Today, that may not be the case. As the management of ICANN proposed a new structure, Dr. David Farber, a respected academic who was involved in the design of the naming and numbering system, and others have raised the possibility of removing the powers of ICANN to another technical organization. In fact, the proposal would resurrect some of Dr. Postel's hegemony.[103]

Another scenario that is unique to the Internet is the possible addition of new names through existing ISPs. I consider this scenario a threat of competitors of specific power, not general power. The competitors' investment or sunken costs in the market for specific power are the costs of establishing a coalition aimed at the specific power, or a credible threat to the exercise (or non-exercise) of that specific power. As in the case of the commercial markets, the market for power, in which ICANN operates, is populated by different actors with different entry costs. They may exert political power, form coalitions or offer rich revenues. Their sunken costs need not be higher than ICANN's entry costs, or may be lower, especially in the case of special powers.

The exit costs of such competitors should be close to zero if their investments can be used elsewhere. However, once a power structure is established, the very loss of the power is not a zero loss even if the coalition can continue to exist and flex its muscle, for example, by entering ICANN's power structure. The investment in creating a competitor to ICANN may be high, because the powerful interests that are potential competitors conflict, and the competitors would be successful only if they find a better way to complement their interests than the one found by ICANN.[104]

103 See ICANN "A Failure" Says ICANN, Newswire (VNU), Mar. 19, 2002, LEXIS, News Library, News Group File.

104 While outsiders who wish to get into the ISP and registry business and increase the number of domain names may try to form such a coalition, they will have to overcome the power of the governments and those who would oppose the extension, as well as those who would be concerned about the stability of the Internet. Thus, it may well be that those who wish to enter the field with two roots will have higher costs than those who would wish to replace ICANN with one root only.

Otherwise, potential competitors would enter the market only if ICANN exerts a higher degree of power than they would together. If ICANN increases or extends its power, competitors may invest in entering the market to enjoy the benefits of the greater power until it will dilute by the mere existence of the competition. Then they will exit, as the exit costs are not high for them.

D. Differences Between Business and Power Markets

One difference between the business market and the power market is that potential competitors can constrain ICANN's power exercise not only by threatening to assert their own claims to power, but also by withdrawing their support of ICANN. A monopolist in the business market does not need the support of its competitors—he receives the support from the consumers. A monopolist in the power market may need that support, and ICANN needs it. Withdrawal involves no direct cost to competitors, but it may be very costly if it undermines ICANN and produces a worse alternative.[105]

Further, while in the business market competitors threaten to offer a competing product, in the power market competitors can threaten to exert power with respect to one special "power product." If ICANN attempts to exercise power that competitors deem to provide "higher rents," these competitors may enter the market, but only in the area requiring low—or no—investment (they already have the power), and where exit is costless (they will exercise the power elsewhere), while the benefit from entry provides high rents. It is harder in the power market to calculate a quantifiable price in terms of power that a monopolist should "charge." Even in the business market this determination has raised a debate. In the power market one can only speculate.

E. When Competitors Will Cooperate

The contestable market theory is not helpful to predict ICANN's evolution if its competitors cooperate, and this possibility is not negligible. Presumably, cooperation among the competitors should be encouraged. It is then renamed a consensus. In fact, the proposed restructure of ICANN seems to be heading towards such

---

105 ICANN may refrain from exercising its power, for example, to establish additional domain names opening the doors to new businesses. Potential competitors may form coalitions to overcome the inaction, and ICANN may take steps to stymie their efforts.market this determination has raised a debate. In the power market one can only speculate.

a coalition and power sharing. A broad-based participation within ICANN signifying a broad-based consensus could lend ICANN legitimacy. Its monopoly power will be constrained from within, as the different interests negotiate. To this extent, ICANN may resemble a policy-making legislative body.

However, legislatures are elected. ICANN is a not-for-profit organization. The power of elected bodies is bestowed on them by the votes. Therefore, elected members must account for their actions to those who bestowed the power on them—the voters. The assets of a not-for-profit corporation are donated usually by its directors (or the directors' designates). They exercise their management power with a sense of entitlement that their donations give them. Theirs is not a legal duty to account to others; theirs is a duty to account to their conscience. This is ICANN's deepest and most serious dilemma.

IV. CONCLUSION

This Article focused on balance of power and structure. It said very little about the crucial component of legitimacy. An organization that lacks clear support of law in a country, lacks a vote of a democratic body politic, lacks a theoretical following of professionals and lacks a popular trust is vulnerable. It is unclear whether political strategies and machinations will sustain it for long. What this Article discusses is another form of sustenance that does not depend on legitimacy but on raw containment of power. Such containment may not be long-term because the actions of the participants are based on self-interest rather than self-governing principles. Its power does not rest on the rule of consensus except the consensus to rule. Whether this base will be sufficient for longevity remains to be seen. On the other hand, if ICANN becomes a platform for negotiations among the interested parties, and in time facilitates the development of acceptable rules and consensus, it will have become a most impressive and unique success.

In a very insightful book, RULING THE WAVES, Debora L. Spar suggests that significant innovations pass through four stages.[106] They first introduce chaos.[107] Next, from the chaos there emerge rules and some patterns of behavior.[108] Eventually, these patterns

---

106 *See* Debora L. Spar, RULING THE WAVES 11-22 (2001).

107 *See id.* at 11-12.

108 *See id.* at 12-15.

form institutions.[109] Finally, and surprisingly, the institutions begin to look and behave as familiar institutions serving the same purposes through and with the aid of the new technology.[110] ICANN may be a very good test case for this prediction. The naming and numbering system has passed through a chaotic stage, emerging as ICANN with rules that are resisted in part, and evolving into an institution. The last stage of "globalization" and the Internet naming system may be grounded in the states or federations of states representing the political systems. Accountability, community values and public interest will return to their rightful position. Business and technical interests will find their voice, but it will not be the dominant voice. We may thus return to the basic form of civic organization, adding to it the Internet service with sufficient links to the rest of the world. Then we could say that there is nothing new under the sun.

---

109 *See id.* at 15-18.

110 *See id.* at 18-22.

Trusting and Non-Trusting on the Internet

101

Trusting and Non-Trusting on the Internet[*]

Tamar Frankel

Introduction

The Puzzle: The Internet is a wonderful innovation, allowing people around the world to communicate, trade, and obtain services. Convenient and rich in choices and opportunities, the Internet is tremendously attractive to buyers. Naturally, businesses are flocking to the Internet. The warning has been sounded that those who do not stake a claim in this incredible new communication medium will be left behind to perish. Yet, with all the enthusiasm, many buyers hesitate to take a serious plunge. Businesses are told repeatedly that they must obtain their customers' trust, yet find it more difficult to gain this trust in cyberspace than in real space. Trust has become a serious stumbling block to developing e-commerce (electronic commerce).

Why is trust so important? How does trust in cyberspace differ from trust in real space? And, if it is important, how can businesses become trusted? This article addresses these questions.

The discussion is framed in terms of the benefits, costs, and risks of trusting relationships, and the mechanisms that reduce the costs and risks of trusting. What is trusting? Trusting is a relationship[1] among individuals, entities and institutions, involving a (i) reasonable belief,

---

[*]   Tamar Frankel, *Trusting and Non-Trusting on the Internet*, 81 B.U.L. Rev. 457 (2001), *available at* https://people.bu.edu/tfrankel/Publications.htm. Reprinted with permission from Boston University School of Law.

1   *See* Rajeev Bhattacharya et al., *A Formal Model of Trust Based on Outcomes, in* 23 The Academy of Mgmt. Rev., Special Forum on Trust in and Between Organizations, 460 (Sim B. Sitkin et al. eds., 1998) (showing that the main view of trusting is a relationship among individuals and groups and rejecting the view that trust is merely an individual trait). Trust is defined as expected behavior of the other party and readiness to risk disappointment. The issue of trusting can be raised only in the context of interaction with others. *See id.*

supported by an acceptable level of verification[2] in (ii) another party's assertion of past facts, present facts, and future facts (promises).[3] Trust in persons, institutions, and society is not blind; it emerges with proof.[4] Gullibility, hope, and faith are relatives of trusting,[5] but reflect different degrees of the actors' requirements for verification.[6] Reasonable belief should depend on the context of the relationship.

2   Some authors add an emotional bond or moral internal drive as a bridge from evidence to belief. *See* Trudy Govier, SOCIAL TRUST AND HUMAN COMMUNITIES 24 (1997) ("Cognitively . . . trust is based on a chosen 'leap' from considered evidence to belief beyond what that evidence would warrant;" that leap is based on an emotional bond among the actors). These elements have merit, but I omit them to simplify the analysis. Further, scholars have defined the risk of trusting as asymmetrical information among the parties, though I decline to add this factor. No two parties have symmetrical information; therefore, risk exists in any human relationship. The risk of trusting relates to the cost of obtaining the relevant information and the degree of assurance that the information is true.

3   There are numerous definitions of trust. For a survey and proposed definition by outcome, *see* Rajeev Bhattacharya et al., *A Formal Model of Trust Based on Outcomes, in* 23 THE ACADEMY OF MGMT. REV., SPECIAL FORUM ON TRUST IN AND BETWEEN ORGANIZATIONS, 460 (Sim B. Sitkin et al. eds., 1998). (listing dictionary definitions of trust and distinguishing among cognitive, emotional and behavioral components of trust). Webster's Dictionary defines trust as the "firm belief or confidence in the honesty, integrity, reliability, justice, etc. of another person or thing." WEBSTER'S NEW WORLD DICTIONARY OF AMERICAN ENGLISH 1436 (3d ed. 1994).

4   *See* Trudy Govier, Social Trust and Human Communities 153 (1997) (discussing social trust as social capital, a resource which emerges with experience). *See also* Ann Marie Zak et al., Assessments of Trust in Intimate Relationships and Self-Perception Process, 138(2) J. Soc. Psych. 217, 225 (1998) (finding that the trusting behavior of the participants in the experiments is often self fulfilling and explaining that blind trust is usually a product of one's self perception). Trustworthy people are more likely to blindly trust others. *See id.*

5   Trusting does not mean believing *all* unverified representations; rather it means believing unverified representations when it is not unreasonable to do so. "[B]elieving when most people of the same social group would consider belief naive and foolish" qualifies as gullibility. *See* Rotter, J. B., 35 Interpersonal Trust, Trustworthiness, and Gullibility, Am. Psych. 1, 4 (1980).

6   Gullibility is an unreasonable belief, as the famous story of the sale of the Brooklyn Bridge demonstrates. Hope involves a strong component of wishing for a future event. A wise person may observe that "a second marriage is a triumph of hope over experience." Notwithstanding experience, the second marriage reflects the parties' hope that, with different spouses and maturity, the second marriage will work. In faith, the quantum of direct evidence is not as relevant to the believer. *But see* Trudy Govier, SOCIAL TRUST AND HUMAN COMMUNITIES 14 (1997) (criticizing the distinction between faith as "an

Reliability in love does not necessarily mean reliability in business relationships, and vice versa. The scope of deeper trust, such as trust in a doctor, lawyer, or priest, is usually limited to particular areas of knowledge or brands of honesty. Further, reasonable belief can be established by verifying the trustworthiness of the other party or by resorting to other sources. The choice of sources often depends on their relative costs.

Cultural norms shape the parameters of reasonableness of the belief. Reasonableness may differ depending on whether the norm is lying, frankness, or vagueness.[7] The law both affects and is affected by these norms. Moreover, trusting is a reflexive and reciprocal relationship.[8] Trusting often creates pressure on trusted persons to meet the expectations of the trusting parties. Signals of mistrust breed rnistrust.[9] Dirty tricks invite reciprocal dirty tricks. As compared to verification cost in real space, verification cost on the Internet is higher. Businesses must learn how to establish trust in the new communication medium.[10] Some believe that the Internet is a free space that should not, and cannot, be regulated,

---

undoubting, unconditional belief in which data for proof and refutation is ignored" and trust as undoubting belief that does not ignore pertinent proof).

7   *See* Trudy Govier, SOCIAL TRUST AND HUMAN COMMUNITIES 230 (1997) (*citing* Sissela Bok, A STRATEGY FOR PEACE (1989)). "Do it yourself" verification may be less costly and more reliable than verification by others. But that is not always true. Cost depends on the "doer's" time value and lost opportunities, as compared to the compensation of experts and agency costs of delegation. For example, the decision would be made depending on which of the following costs exceed the others: the cost of "do it yourself" (X (acquiring expertise) + Y (lost opportunities)) or the cost of delegating verification to others (A (compensation to the delegate) + B (agency costs)). Thus, one's own judgment may be decisive because one bears the consequences of the decision, but one's level of wisdom, knowledge and expertise, may be lower. Though people ask for the opinions of others, they ultimately make up their own minds.

8   *See* Trudy Govier, SOCIAL TRUST AND HUMAN COMMUNITIES 27 (1997) (asserting that trust is a reflexive phenomenon; to be trusted requires having trust).

9   *See id.* at 87-88 (attempt of teachers in a Canadian law school to control students through minutely detailed rules of examinations led to a culture of mistrust; the attitude of mistrust bred more mistrust).

10   *See* John O. Whitney, THE ECONOMICS OF TRUST: LIBERATING PROFITS AND RESTORING CORPORATE VITALITY (1996) (creating trusting within the organization and with outside parties is profitable as well as good); Roderick M. Kramer and Tom R. Tyler, TRUST IN ORGANIZATIONS, FRONTIERS OF THEORY AND RESEARCH 232 (1996) (showing the many ways in which trust is important to organizational life including business organizations; noting that trust is based in reciprocity and is tied to one's expectations).

and that markets can resolve the trusting problem. I argue that without the bedrock of legitimizing law, trusting on the Internet will not develop. To be sure, market regulated actors on the Internet must occupy the first line of enforcement. Internet, and perhaps also real space, activities are policed by private sector institutions and professional gatekeepers. To be effective and legitimate, such police must be regulated especially when their interests conflict with the interests of those whom they are required to protect. The law not only punishes breach of trust; it also provides trusted persons with a reputation, which they value personally and professionally. Further, the law can enhance the norm of trustworthiness and increase social trust.

Because building trusting relationships through the Internet is in the making, we can only speculate on how the process will ultimately mature. Mechanisms to establish trust, however, have been emerging. Not surprisingly, they are mostly the same mechanisms used in real space, which are adjusted to the new Internet environment. The role of the law in this adjustment is unclear. While we start from known rules and approaches, new law making and law enforcement techniques may develop. Further, domestic laws and norms may spill over to other countries, interacting with their laws and norms. A question regarding the role of the law has appeared in connection with parties' choices in designing the rules that govern their relationships. The process by which legal systems interact has also appeared in the context of regulating areas such as money laundering and insider trading.

The Internet may lead to different line drawing, in light of the different constraints, freedoms, and enforcement techniques that the Internet offers. However, I believe that with respect to trusting and verification the parties will continue to seek the least costly verification and the highest benefits from interaction. Therefore, the law will continue to provide and strengthen the norms for self-enforcement and legitimacy for verifiers. This law may not necessarily be domestic law supported by a political or international force. It may be enforced in other ways. Because people will feel constrained to follow it, it will be legitimate law. If law's support of norms and verifiers remains weak, the cost of trusting will dissipate its benefits and the hope that the Internet holds for a more productive and cohesive world is not likely to materialize.

I. TRUSTING AND NON-TRUSTING: RELATIVE COSTS, BENEFITS, AND RISKS

Trusting involves costs, benefits, and risks to both the trusted and the trusting parties. The division of these components among the parties is difficult to establish because the parties can transfer the costs and benefits between each other. Therefore, it is easier to speak of these costs, benefits, and risks in the aggregate. Viewed separately, however, if the risks and costs of reducing the risks to the *trusting* party are higher than the benefits, the party will not interact. If the costs to the *trusted* party of establishing its trustworthiness are higher than the benefits, it will not interact. The parties will enter into a relationship, however, if third parties, including the government through the law, reduces their costs, bridging the gap. As discussed later, these third parties are usually institutions and intermediaries whose trustworthiness is backed by law.

A trusting person can verify facts and promises from the trusted party or other alternative sources. The differences in verification costs are greatly affected by the number of the interactions among the parties. Establishing trustworthiness of another is costly. However, once the other party is proven trustworthy, there is no need to verify its statements of facts or its promises, even if some monitoring is required.[11] When negotiating with the Russians, during the Cold War, President Reagan used the phrase: "Trust, but verify."[12] This statement drew chuckles because if the other party is trusted, there is no need to verify its statements and promises. The need to prove truthfulness of facts and reliability of promises signifies absence of trust in the other party.

---

11 Some cultures focus on the identity of counter parties. They decline to do business with foreigners, members outside the family group, or another race, or strangers unless introduced by reliable friends. The quantum and sources of evidence form the measures of reasonableness of belief on which trusting is based. One can reasonably believe statements made by a trusted person, similar to indirect evidence. One can reasonably believe in the reliability of promises by trusting the promisor on the basis of the promisor's character, reputation, and past performance. Independent verification, such as proof by documents or independent parties, (e.g., accountants, lawyers, independent witnesses, or experts, or guarantors) may support the trustworthiness of the trusted party.

12 Associated Press, *Historic Missile Treaty Signed; Leaders Pledge Further Efforts for Arms Control*, L.A. TIMES, Dec. 8, 1987, *at* A1.

For example, if the cost of verifying a fact and a promise is $X, and the relationship (with one or more persons) involves Y facts and promises, a non trusting party would have to spend $XY to verify. A trusting party would have to spend $0. A greater number of transactions among parties render trusting increasingly cheaper than non-trusting. For the non-trusting party, the cost rises by the magnitude of XY with each transaction. For the trusting party, the cost remains close to zero. The cost of establishing trusting-$E-should be now added. For the non-trusting party (that verifies from outside sources) the cost of establishing trusting is zero. Monitoring is our next item-$M. In each case, monitoring is a function of the risks from the relationship. The higher the risk, the higher the monitoring cost would be. I assume that in non-trusting relationships, the risk from the relationship is Z% and the cost of monitoring is $MZ. In trusting relationships, the risk from the relationship is W% and the costs of monitoring is $MW. In sum, to determine the relative costs of trusting and non-trusting we may use this crude formula: For trusting parties: E (cost of establishing the relationship) + MW (cost of monitoring determined by the level of risk). For non-trusting parties: XY (cost of verifying each fact and promise) + MZ (cost of monitoring determined by the level of risk).[13]

In general, after the initial investment in establishing the relationship, personal trusting offers the parties the benefits of lower risks and information costs.[14] Further, trust can substitute for and reduce the costs of formal contracts. There is evidence that in trusting relationships people forego costly formal contracts. There are corporations that do business only on a handshake, although they are usually relatively small.[15] Also,

---

[13] This analysis is similar to Coase's *Theory of the Firm*. A firm can be viewed as an organizational form that enhances trusting, thereby reducing costs of interaction. If contracts were adequate, the firm would not be necessary. This argument was suggested by Professor Michael Meurer.

[14] *See* Richard A. Posner, Economic Analysis of Law 284 (5th ed. 1998) ("Honesty, trustworthiness, and love reduce the costs of transactions."). There is also the psychological benefit of simplified complex information. Social trusting, that is trusting by a large group governed by similar trusting norms, can also enhance economic prosperity.

[15] *See* Juliet P. Kostritsky, *Bargaining With Uncertainty, Moral Hazard, and Sunk Costs: A Default Rule For Precontractual Negotiations*, 44 Hastings L.J. 621, 643 (1993) (noting that trust may substitute for legal formalities, such as contracts, in on-going relationships); Michael Meyer, *Here's a "Virtual" Model for America's Industrial Giants*, Newsweek, Aug. 1993, *at* 40 (describing Kingston

in trusting relationships, the parties are unlikely to face the Prisoner's Dilemma.[16] This classic dilemma shows that reasoning from self-interest can be self-defeating.[17] Finally, trusting arguably benefits the economy. Even if we view the world as an association of individuals, their survival depends on each other. A measure of trusting must be forged among us, or we will die.

Technology Corporation and its lack of formal dealing). "Trust cements the network. It is the essence of our relationships The deals were closed on a handshake, Kingston style." *Id.* (internal quotation marks omitted).

16 *See* Robert Cooter & Thomas Ulen, Law and Economics 93 n.3 (2000) (describing the Prisoner's Dilemma as a non-cooperative game). In this game, two suspects are kept incommunicado in different prison cells, and offered the following: if one confesses and the other does not, the confessor received half a year in prison and the non-confessor ten years. If both confess, each receives 5 years. If neither confesses, each receives one year. Their best bet is not to confess, but that depends on whether the other will. *See id.* Most terms of the bargain remain implicit anyway, regardless of how detailed contracts are. It is often more efficient to deal with another party that tends to reach working solutions and shares a similar sense of fairness than with a party that "goes by the (contract) book." In a trust relationship, the parties know approximately what each can be expected to do in the case of misunderstanding, and are willing to take the risk that the result will not be satisfactory. That risk taking is not only reasonable but is likely to be cost-saving.

17 *See* Trudy Govier, Social Trust and Human Communities 11 (1997) (The Prisoner's Dilemma "serves to indicate the self-defeating character of the single-minded and solitary pursuit of one's own self-interest."). Another benefit from trusting is demonstrated in the workplace. Recently, American businesses have worked hard to create trusting and cooperation among their employees, and between employees and management. Far more discretion has been vested in employees. A similar pattern of limited cooperation among competing business organizations is also developing. *See* John O. Whitney, The Economics of Trust: Liberating Profits and Restoring Corporate Vitality 191 (1996) (arguing that creating a trusting environment within the organization and outside is both profitable and good); *Special Forum on Trust in and Between Organizations*, 23 Academy of Mgmt. Rev. 459 (Sim B. Sitkin et al. eds., 1998) (containing papers on trust building and its benefits in business organizations and defining trust using mathematical models). *See also* Bruce Chapman, *Trust, Economic Rationality, and the Corporate Fiduciary Obligation*, 43 U. Toronto L.J. 547 (1993) (arguing against the concept of a corporation as a contract and emphasizing the role of trust and loyalty in the corporate organization); Giancarlo Spangnolo, *Social Relationships and Cooperation in Organizations*, 38 J. Economic Behavior & Organization 1 (1999) (addressing "the effects of social relationships on cooperation (or collusion) in organizations (or communities) "and arguing that the employment of members of the same community facilitates cooperation in production and increases social capital because "the linkage generates transfers of 'trust'").

There are indications that social trusting is crucial to economic prosperity, and perhaps, the very existence of individuals and society.[18] Specialization is a necessary component of a prosperous economy. Specialization requires interdependence, which cannot exist without a measure of trusting.[19] In an entirely non-trusting relationship, interaction would be too expensive and too risky to maintain.[20] There is a correlation between the level of trusting relationships on which members of a society operate and the level of that society's trade and economic prosperity.[21]

On the Internet, there are similar benefits, costs, and risks from trusting. The balance among the trusting and trusted,

18 *See* Trudy Govier, SOCIAL TRUST AND HUMAN COMMUNITIES 153 (1997) ("For politics, economics, and personal well-being, social trust is a valuable resource."). Social capital is defined as a moral resource and a public good that is self-perpetuating and lubricates the growth of trust in society. *See id.* Lack of trust is costly in psychological terms. The unknown is risky; it breeds fear and anxiety, which can be debilitating. *See* Niklas Luhmann, TRUST AND POWER 4 (1980), *quoted in* Bernard Barber, THE LOGIC AND LIMITS OF TRUST, 10 (1983) ("'But a complete absence of trust would prevent him even from getting up in the morning. He would be prey to a vague sense of dread, to paralyzing fears. He would not even be capable of formulating distrust and making that a basis for precautionary measures, since this would presuppose trust in other directions. Anything and everything would be possible. Such abrupt confrontation with the complexity. of the world at its most extreme is beyond human endurance.'"). *See also* Lawrence E. Mitchell, *Fairness and Trust in Corporate Law*, 43 DUKE L.J. 425, 432-33 (1993) (noting that the destruction of trust would be the "destruction of the possibility of social relations").

19 *See* Trudy Govier, SOCIAL TRUST AND HUMAN COMMUNITIES 26 (1997) (noting the element of vulnerability required to trust in matters with which we are unfamiliar). In complex societies we need to trust many people, including experts on information that we do not understand, even if it were disclosed to us. *See id.*; Tamar Frankel, *Fiduciary Law*, 71 CAL. L. REV. 795, 803-04 (1983) (discussing specialization and its relation to fiduciary law; specialization is the most efficient way to utilize knowledge)."

20 Nature's world is no different; sharks are one of the few exceptions. *See Behavior, formerly at* http://www.seaworld.org/sharks/behavior.html (noting that sharks are basically asocial).

21 *See* Francis Fukuyama, TRUST: THE SOCIAL VIRTUES AND THE CREATION OF PROSPERITY 7 (1995) (noting that a nation's ability to compete is conditioned by the level of trust inherent in the society); Francis Fukuyama, GREAT DISRUPTION: HUMAN NATURE AND THE RECONSTITUTION OF SOCIAL ORDER 256 (1999) (defining attributes such as honesty and fairness as social capital, produced by private markets to increase profits); John O. Whitney, THE ECONOMICS OF TRUST: LIBERATING PROFITS AND RESTORING CORPORATE VITALITY (1996) (asserting that trusting is profitable as well as good); Bruce Chapman, *Trust, Economic Rationality, and the Corporate Fiduciary Obligation*, 43 U. TORONTO L.J. 547 (1993).

however, is different than the balance in real space. Sellers on the Internet can benefit from increased number of customers and revenues and decreased costs of real space storage. and inventory. Moreover, the sellers' risks are no higher than their risks in real space and may even be lower (e.g., robbery). Hence, it pays to do business through the Internet and expend more resources to gain the customers' trust.

Benefits to shoppers on the Internet are also higher than in real space in terms of savings of time. Costs of verification, however, render their risks far higher. While it opens connections to the world, the Internet allows relatively few signals that support trustworthiness to pass through. In fact, it enables people to create virtual worlds, personalities, and products that do not materialize. Customers' cost-benefit analysis suggests that the convenience of Internet shopping is significantly reduced by its risks.

In general, it is costly to persuade others of one's trustworthiness. A new relationship may bloom over time into a trusting relationship. In both trust and non-trust, uncertainty and risk are reduced with experience.[22] Verification depends on past, and frequency of, experience. People are creatures of habit; habits are long-term and personality traits are life-long. In personal relationships, it is easier to discover whether the other party can perform her promises, has the necessary money or product, or possesses the requisite skill.[23] One detects signals attributed to general character traits, such as responsiveness, dependability, and honesty.[24] During the process, people offer reciprocal reassurance and accommodation, as well as joint monitoring which reduces the risk of disappointed expectations.[25] As nothing is certain, however, efforts to fully rely on another may fail. Notwithstanding the tendency to repeat patterns of behavior, a trusted party may change, for example, with age or illness, marriage, or great

---

22 *See* Trudy Govier, Social Trust and Human Communities 6 (1997) (noting that the degree of trust increases with positive interactions, and decreases with negative interactions).

23 *But see* Rolf Ziegler, Trust and the Reliability of Expectations, Rationality and Society 427 (1998) ("In the short run, an actor may decide to raise his forecasting ability by increased but costly attention, but in the medium run it can only be improved by learning processes.").

24 *See* John G. Holmes & John K. Rempel, Close Relationships 187, 192 (Clyde Hendrick ed. 1989), citing Kelly & Stahelsk, 1970; Miller & Holmes, 1975.

25 *See id.*

temptation. The trustworthiness of an institution may change with changing control and different key personnel.

To establish and maintain personal trusting is costly also in terms of lost opportunities. A person can interact with a limited number of people. There are even fewer persons with whom the interaction can be long-term. Usually people in poor societies limit their business interaction to family, which limits their ability to recruit talent for their businesses.[26] Families with many children may maintain thriving businesses for generations if some of the children continue to develop the family business. But limiting the leadership of a business to family members puts the business at a competitive disadvantage that, at some point, may lead to its demise.[27] Thus, establishment and maintenance of personal trust involves lost opportunities for individuals and businesses.

One effective mechanism that reduces the cost and risks of personal trusting is the utilization of trusted legitimate institutions and intermediaries, both private and public. Institutions reduce trusting costs regardless of consumers' culture and regardless of whether personal trust is mixed with skepticism. For example, Americans revere their Constitution and the rules of law. They trust their banks, mutual funds, and insurance companies and the legal controls under which these institutions are made trustworthy. Americans have a reasonable belief in these institutions. On the personal side of the same coin, Americans have a significant degree of what some would call healthy skepticism in their politicians, lawyers, bankers, and mutual fund money managers. The argument that institutions have no identity because they are merely composed of individuals is flawed. Institutions have a personality apart from the people who compose them. This personality is comprised of their internal structures, rules, leadership, and their relationships among their staff as well as with the outside world. Institutions have a history and a reputation for competence and honesty (or the reverse) which they can build or

26 *See* Francis Fukuyama, TRUST: THE SOCIAL VIRTUES AND THE CREATION OF PROSPERITY 78-79 (1995) (noting that Chinese, unlike American entrepreneurial families, are likely to remain small and internally managed due to distrust of outsiders).

27 *See id.* (noting that distrust of non-family members usually prevents institutionalization of Chinese businesses and drawing on outside talent). When trusting relationships have evolved not within the family but within a large work place, the work place is sufficiently large to maintain and nurture talent.

destroy.[28] Institutions send, in their unique ways, their brand of signals that can evoke trust or mistrust. Distinguished from their members, truth-telling institutions, which honor their promises, will be trusted, as will the persons who act on their behalf.[29] Others will not.[30]

The benefits of institutional or impersonal trusting are very great. People can trade with strangers through trusted intermediaries and institutions based on impersonal trust.[31] The

---

28 Note the following two examples: In the 1950s, an aggressive and successful young underwriting firm, Otis & Co, reneged on its underwriting obligations on the ground that the issuer did not provide accurate information in its prospectus. The huge potential liability caused Otis to petition for bankruptcy protection. *See Bankruptcy Referee Asks Court Dismiss Reorganization Plan*, N.Y. TIMES, Dec. 9, 1992, *at* 53. The company was put up for sale even before the final decision. *See Otis to Consider Offers for its Retail Business*, N.Y. TIMES, July 28, 1951, *at* 17. Otis won the case. *See Kaiser-Frazer Corp. v. Otis & Co.*, 195 F.2d 838 (2d Cir.), *cert. denied,* 344 U.S. 856 (1952) (defendants won because contract at issue was unenforceable and prospectus misrepresentation was illegal under securities laws). The management of Salomon Brothers turned its attention away from employees that violate the law but brought substantial profits. *See* John H. Gutfreund, Exchange Act Release No. 31,554 (Dec. 3, 1992). Even though it settled the charges against it, it lost its independence five years thereafter to Travelers. *See* Thomas S. Mulligan, *Travelers to Buy Salomon Bros. for $9 Billion*, L.A. TIMES, Sept. 25, 1997 *at* Al, Al2. After the 1991 scandal, Salomon was "financially crippled" and sold to Warran Buffet. When the company was sold again in 1997, a commentator noted that it "never really regained (its) position" after the scandal. *Id.*

29 *See* Trudy Govier, SOCIAL TRUST AND HUMAN COMMUNITIES 206 (1997) (noting that public perceptions of leaders of an organization reflect upon the individual members; this is exemplified by the widespread use of advertising).

30 For centuries, intermediaries have served to reduce the cost of trusting relationships among strangers. Financial intermediaries earned their keep by creating trusting relationships with customers, and enforcing promises among strangers. For example, the Rothschilds have facilitated trusting relationships by inter-positioning themselves among unknown parties, and offering a competent family network backed by substantial capital. Likewise, banks have offered letters of credit to establish a trusting relationship among traders in different lands. Purchases by catalogs are made possible by the inter-positioning of banks and credit card banking associations. The securities markets would not exist without the inter-positioning of brokers and dealers, who ensure execution of transactions among strangers in volatile markets. While it is likely that one of the parties will renege on the trade, the intermediary has an interest in executing the transaction because that is when the intermediary receives his compensation. Very few trades are litigated for breach. Intermediaries perform similar functions in other markets.

31 In comparing American impersonal trusting with Japanese personal trusting, one can see the weakness of the Japanese system. The focal point

relative costs of personal trusting described above involve sunken costs (long-term repeat relationships that may also prove to be disappointing), lost opportunities (limiting the range of human interaction both in number and geographically), and monitoring. In comparison, trust in institutions and intermediaries are cheaper to establish.

First, the number of institutions is smaller than the number of people with whom business can be conducted, a factor that reduces the investment in verifying the trustworthiness of the institutions. In addition, buyers, investors, borrowers, and depositors can move from one institution to another with little cost.[32]

Second, institutions have relative longevity, and can build impressive reputations, both positive and negative.[33] Thus, there are little sunken costs in establishing trusting relationships with institutions such as banks or large retailers. Establishing impersonal trust in them is therefore less expensive.

Third, institutions reduce lost opportunities of interacting with strangers,[34] allowing people to deal with strangers and benefit from services of capable strangers who function under the umbrella of the institutions.[35] Thus, like all intermediaries, the costs of establishing the truthfulness and reliability of the strangers and employees are borne by the institutions at costs lower than the costs to the individual customers.

Fourth, and most importantly, risks from trusting commercial and financial institutions are reduced by law. The institutions are

---

of this weakness is with regard to financial institutions, which Japan is now remodeling. In an international economy, impersonal trusting has become crucial to national economic prosperity.

32 For example, many state laws prohibit banks from penalizing borrowers who wish to refinance mortgages (that is, pay off their mortgage loans and take loans at lower interest).

33 *See* Trudy Govier, SOCIAL TRUST AND HUMAN COMMUNITIES 153 (1997). Social trust is based on the experience of individuals and groups. People involved in associations are not likely to let others down, for their personal reputations would suffer if they did. "For politics, economics, and personal well-being, social trust is a valuable resource." *Id.*

34 *See id.* (contrasting modern trust in institutions with Swedish village life where consumers only transact with known merchants). A sociologist "ties modern trust more to people's sense of how institutions operate than to their attitudes towards unknown individuals." *Id.*

35 *See id.* at 29 ("To live in a complex society without going mad, we must have trust in systems too.").

strictly regulated and surrounded by substantial guarantees against misfortune. All of these benefits are too costly for individuals to ensure through self-help. This role of the law in strengthening trusting relationships is described in section III below.

On the Internet, verification of trustworthy persons, on the one hand, and facts and promises, on the other hand, is more costly for the trusting person as compared to those in real space. The Internet exposes buyers to greater misinformation for it is technically easier to show on the Internet items that look real but are not. In real space, one can judge a store by its location, appearance, customers, and many other signals. On the Internet, one can show a beautiful store that does not exist, hide information about people, and disseminate more misinformation. There is neither body language nor voice signals to guide the viewer, for today the printed word is the main medium of Internet communication.[36]

Thus, situations that do not require trusting and involve low or no verification costs involve higher costs on the Internet. In real space, the purchaser of a newspaper bears little or no cost in verifying the newspaper and its price, and no promise is involved because the exchange is simultaneous. Transactions on the Internet are not simultaneous. A newspaper purchase involves higher costs of verifying that the newspaper ordered, especially if paid for in advance, will be delivered on time. Thus, on the Internet, both the costs of verifying statements and promises in non-trusting relationships, and the cost of establishing personal relationships and verifying trustworthiness are likely to be higher than in real space. These high costs are evidenced by the new third parties that provide verification services regarding transactions and actors on the Internet, while none of such services are offered in real space. All these services come at a cost.

Risks from third parties undermines consumers' trust in the Internet. Consumers who provide sellers with credit card and other information are exposed to an additional risk that the information will be misappropriated and abused. Under United States law, if stolen credit cards are used for unauthorized purchases, banks or sellers must indemnify consumers for losses above $50. But on

---

36 Most business relationships on the Internet today do not involve the offer and receipt of personal services, such as medical and legal services, which must involve a higher level of trusting than purchasing goods. Through the Internet, trading transactions are more costly and riskier than in real space for the same reasons that medical and legal services are costlier in real space.

the Internet, consumers may not know that their card numbers have been stolen because they still hold their cards. If the thieves change the account addresses and the consumers fail to notice that they did not receive bills, consumers may not notify the bank of the loss of the cards. They will be personally liable and their credit will be destroyed.

Third parties harm consumers by malicious hyper-links and "spamming"—an avalanche of advertising causing bottlenecks on consumers' computers. Technology provides some redress from these harms, at a cost, and only temporarily, until spammers have designed software to circumvent the protections. Congress, however, is acting on this issue.[37]

Credit cards and debit cards are useful devices that expose customers to risks. The cards resemble letters of credit that were established through banks hundreds of years ago to facilitate trading among strangers in different countries. Sellers are not willing to take the risk of payment after sending the sold products. At the same time, buyers have the option of contesting the charges and that constitutes the banks as arbitrators of a dispute between the parties.

The value of the cards to both parties gives the banks enforcement powers, provided they follow fair and unbiased procedure. These procedures are subject to regulation, and banks have self-interest in following them to gain lucrative, trust-based business. This mechanism, however, exposes customers and sellers to risk from third parties. Personal and financial information may be stolen from sellers, exposing customers to loss of property, and sellers to extortion. If sellers refuse to pay, the thieves publish the customers' card numbers. Further, like customers, businesses suffer from spamming bottlenecks, called "denial of service." Businesses also suffer from the spread of lies and gossip about their products.

Finally, businesses that are expending funds and efforts to build reputation may be hurt from the misdeeds of a few "bad apples," especially newcomers to the industry, if seed capital is small. If some of these newcomers are dishonest, they can deplete the wealth of social trusting that society and most businesses have developed.

In addition, traditional policing and enforcement against illegal actions is weaker on the Internet, although the Internet

---

37 *See* Unsolicited Commercial Electronic Mail Act of 2001, H.R. 95, 107th Cong. (2001) (often called the CAN-SPAM Act).

does offer added enforcement tools, including publication and automated monitoring. Thus, both costs and risks for buyers (and some for sellers) on the Internet are higher than in real space. Sooner or later, consumers recognize the danger.[38]

II. RISK REDUCTION

In general, common interests can reduce the risks associated with trusting, as similarity of character can.[39] Parties to a relationship with similar interests and few alternatives are likely to be trustworthy towards each other. The stronger their self-interest in the relationship, the more trustworthy they will be. A relationship, in which at least one party can terminate without serious adverse effects, will have weak interdependence and verification, increasing the likelihood that this party will renege on its promises as more attractive opportunities arise.[40]

Similar incentives operate on the Internet. Information about persons on the other side of an e-mail message is costly to verify, making personal trust building on the Internet better achieved by sharing, as in real space. Groups sharing areas of interest, values, or ideas can build trust relationships among themselves, sometimes to the exclusion of, or even against, others. Anonymity can help shy people be frank. For example, people tend to share their secrets on an airplane ride, when they believe that they will probably never see each other again. Similarly, consumers will likely develop associations on the Internet to share information about products, services, and their own experiences, and such associations will help reduce the risk to buyers.

---

38   Consumers who are not familiar with communicating on the Internet seem to be more gullible than they would be in real space. They view experts in Internet communications as more trustworthy. Thus there is something like a reverse order: expertise produces dependency and dependency produces trust.

39   Russell Hardin defines trust mostly in terms of encapsulated interest. *See* Russell Hardin, *Trust and Trustworthiness*, 81 B.U.L. REV. 495 (2001). I argue that encapsulated interest is a risk-reducing situation that contributes to trusting but is not trusting per se.

40   *See* Diego Gambetia, THE SICILIAN MAFIA: THE BUSINESS OF PRIVATE PROTECTION 28 (1993) ("[G]ood behavior in business evolve(s) from an economic interest in keeping promises and acquiring a reputation for honest dealing. . . . This may also explain why the opposite norm obtains and the ability to cheat is praised and encouraged."). *See also* Russell Hardin, *Trust and Trustworthiness*, 81 B.U.L. REV. 495 (2001) (explaining that our first reaction is to distrust those about whom we have little knowledge).

Proof of one party's trustworthiness, through consistent behavior, can reduce the risks associated with trusting. A similar approach works on the Internet. The Internet site and the brand name have replaced sales persons. The site has become the contact point with the customer; there is no other. The site, however, may be less convincing than a salesperson might be. Therefore, businesses focus on the services they give, by doing it right: they tell the truth and keep their word. Easy access to businesses is essential, but the best advertising for businesses is the actual services that they provide. The model for businesses on the Internet is similar to the model of establishing trusting relationships in real space, especially for professionals and fiduciaries. With time, customers' good experiences establish customers' trust. Because information about bad services can be easily spread, the punishment for being untrustworthy is faster customer withdrawal in even greater numbers than in real space.

Self-help can also reduce the risks associated with trusting. Self-help is very costly on the Internet, even when it is effective in the real world. Despite these costs, the current trend seems to be towards self-protection. Consumers trust other parties less than they would in real space and behave as non-trusting persons would; they require proof of facts and promises and other trust building evidence. Experts advise consumers to engage in costly self-protection. They advise consumers to educate themselves about the risks involving the Internet, to get information about the sellers, to read carefully the small print regarding warranties, to check the security of credit cards and financial information; and to consider alternative options, such as ordering by telephone.

On the Internet, some of the verification costs and burdens have shifted from buyers to sellers. The shift is efficient. First, commercial and financial institutions can reap enormous benefits from Internet communications. Presumably, that gives them incentives to expend more efforts to gain customers' trust. New market entrants, or sellers of new products, recognize the need to capture customers' trust even in real space.

Second, as compared to real space, the level of customers' commitment is not as high. While buyers are exposed to more costs and risks in Internet transactions, buyers have alternatives to buy in real space, even though they lack the convenience and choices of Internet shopping. As their risks and costs have risen, many customers are inclined to expend little effort in reducing their risks. Thus, in relation to verification, the bargaining power between these two groups has changed and shifted from buyers to sellers.

Third, the cost of proof and risk reduction may be lower for the sellers than for the consumers. Although sellers can shift the added costs to consumers, competition limits such increases. Therefore, even if sellers transfer some of the costs, buyers' increased costs will still be lower than if the buyers had to verify the facts and promises themselves. Fourth, the more sellers succeed in convincing customers of their facts and promises, the lower their burden becomes as they build a trusting relationship with their customers.

Finally, many sellers have begun to recognize that they are better off uniting than competing on the issue of trustworthiness. A race to the bottom will bring Internet use to the bottom as well. Therefore, there should be, and hopefully there is, a growing tendency to monitor others, at least in the same industry, to maintain a minimal level of trustworthiness.

Market actors can reduce the risks associated with trusting. Sellers can offer self-binding obligations, such as warranties, and "no questions asked" return policies. Lower information and verification costs can reduce the risks associated with trusting. A reputation for being trustworthy is one such mechanism that businesses can also acquire in the market.[41] Hence, people rely on reputation, good or bad, as a form of verification, as an added comfort or as the least expensive alternative when direct sources of information are too costly. In commerce, it is reasonable to believe that a person's performance will be consistent with his past performance and representations, unless there are indications to the contrary. People are bound by inertia and the pace of change in their behavior is slower that other changes in the environment. Those who are fickle, depending on how closely they are watched,

---

41   Market reputation has a different weight than personal observation, yet can carry weight of the aggregate opinion of others. It is more like price, a "black box," unless others have similar concerns. Reputation is a marketing device, distinguishing competitors in the markets. Trustworthy people offer reduced information costs to other parties, and can therefore charge more for their services and products. When transactions are trust dependent to the extent that most people would not engage in a business relationship without trusting, the assurance of trusting becomes crucial to the transaction. In such a case, the interference of the law as a guarantor of trustworthiness may be cost reducing and even necessary.

are unlikely to become steadfast. Those who are reliable, regardless of whether they are watched are not, are unlikely to become erratic. In terms of learning and prediction, too many drastic changes in behavior are costly to the actors and to those who deal with them. Thus, people develop habits, and believe that others will stick to theirs.

On the Internet, information tools can develop for individuals. For example, direct traders can create a personal business reputation on the Internet, as the eBay[42] experience has shown. Traders on the Internet eBay site are likely to rely on their own experiences, and on those of others regarding other individuals' behavior, and choose their trading partners according to the reputation they developed for telling the truth and keeping their word. The low publication costs, and eBay's services, provide powerful information that helps make or break a reputation fairly quickly. The reputation of traders on eBay's site affects the prices traders can obtain or are willing to pay. A trader with a good reputation will attract more bidders who will bid the price up. A trader with a poor reputation will attract fewer bidders, who will not bid the price for the same item as high.

A reputation-forming device, such as membership in professional and other groups, can also reduce the risks associated with trusting. Membership signifies a high probability that members have passed the requirements of entry into that group, be they educational requirements (e.g., medical), character based requirements (e.g., clergy), or simply acceptance by peers and conformity to the rules of the group (e.g., trade organizations). Thus, accountants, lawyers, physicians, and others command trusting in their competence and honesty. Many groups subscribe to norms that build trustworthiness, and impose on members a duty to enforce the norms, rendering the norms powerful and the members credible.[43]

Internet businesses have followed the real space model, and formed societies whose main function is to gain the customers' trust. Internet businesses recognize that their competitors, who may act unwisely, can adversely affect their own reputation. For

---

42 *See* eBay, *formerly* at http://pages.ebay.com/help/basics/n-is-ebay safe. html (touting site's "built-in safeguards" to ensure buyers and sellers are "honest and reliable").

43 *See* Robert Axelrod, THE COMPLEXITY OF COOPERATION: AGENT-BASED MODELS OF COMPETITION AND COOPERATION 65-66 (1997) (describing metanorms).

example, Financial Services Technology Consortium is composed of competitors, who combine to create a "public good," that is, trustworthiness for all, and monitor their members to maintain this public good.[44]

Markets are populated by private sector professionals and organizations with significant reputations, which act as reliable verifiers of others' assertions of facts and promises. They can verify the information or actually lend their credit and name to back the sellers' obligations. That involvement offers parties both an additional trusted obligor and an indirect assurance of verified information, which the obligor will gather to protect its interests. Accountants and lawyers act as market verifiers of information. They command trust by membership in self-regulating organizations, and by strict government regulation. They verify information about the trustworthiness of strangers.

There are organizations that check businesses for trustworthiness in terms of expertise and proof.[45] Rating agencies perform a similar function. They evaluate bonds after gathering information about issuers including an evaluation of the creditworthiness (trustworthiness) of the issuers. The rating agency, Moody's Investor Service,[46] offers for a fee, "trust packages" to parties who wish to reduce their risk of business relationships with unknown parties abroad. It ascertains whether the unknown party abroad is trustworthy by verifying information, offering the same kind of fact-finding that people engage into develop a trusting relationship. Moody's has developed a list of factors that demonstrate trustworthiness, collects information about the unknown party's consistency in performing its promises, paying its debts, making true statements, and conducting long-term

44 *See Financial Services Technology Consortium*, https://www.datanyze.com/companies/financial-services-technology-consortium/109348040 (last visited Oct. 31, 2023)(comprising 90 organizations working in collaboration to create new methods for "commercial transaction on the Internet").

45 It was suggested that the value of board directorship for busy corporate leaders is in "networking" and current information, including information about other actors in their field.

46 *See* Moody's Investor Service *at* https://www.moodys.com (last visited Aug 15, 2023) (providing "independent credit ratings research and financial information" to help investors analyze credit risks and reduce transaction costs); https://gac.icann.org/principles-and-guidelines/public/principles-cctlds.pdf *at* 7.2.

relationships.[47] In fact, Moody's has commodified, and is selling, trustworthiness.[48]

Internet businesses have followed the same model. The Internet markets have additional third-party fact verifiers, especially when information can be manipulated on the Internet. For example, pictures shown on the Internet can be digitally changed. Third parties can provide verification of products, such as the true color of women's clothes. This verification was adopted as a selling point to consumers who otherwise mistrust the on-line display. Unauthorized persons can alter and sign documents transferred through the Internet. Technology is developing to ensure the integrity of documents and signatures. Third party intermediaries offer trust services for Internet businesses, such as iEscrow escrow services, to ensure that buyers pay money in advance but the money reaches the sellers only upon delivery.

Like reputation building in real space, businesses build their reputation through associations. The United States government offers verification, in the negative sense, about those who are not trustworthy. The Federal Trade Commission issues "Consumer Alerts!" on its on-line web site.[49] Other associations issue positive recommendations about businesses that act on the Internet,

---

47   Banks have offered a similar service in the form of letters of credit since the seventeenth century. The letters of credit, however, provide a guarantee to parties abroad, who do not know, and therefore, do not trust the domestic parties' promises. The bank undertakes, unconditionally, the obligation to pay upon presentation of the bills of lending, providing evidence that the goods have arrived; https://gac.icann.org/principles-and-guidelines/public/principles-cctlds.pdf *at* 7.3.

48   *See* Bernard S. Black & Ronald J. Gilson, *Venture Capital and The Structure of Capital Markets: Banks versus Stock Markets*, 47 J. Fin. Econ. 243, 253 (1998) (stating that venture capital funds have an incentive to "monitor entrepreneurs' performance"). *See also* Symposium, *The Internet and Small Business Capital Formation*, 2 J. Small & Emerging Bus. L. (1998) (stating that venture capital companies also provide a similar, though more intrusive service); Stephen J. Choi, *Gatekeepers and the Internet: Rethinking the Regulations of Small Business Capital Formation*, 2 J. Small & Emerging Bus. L. 27, 45 (1998).

49   *See Federal Trade Commission* (visited March 9, 2001) https://www.ftc.gov (last visited Aug. 15, 2023) ("The FTC works for the consumer to prevent fraudulent, deceptive, and unfair business practices in the marketplace and to provide information to help consumers spot, stop, and avoid them.").

similar to the Better Business Bureau's, such as the Center for Democracy and Technology.[50]

Both on the Internet and in real space, trustworthiness can evaporate on disappointing evidence. But it seems that on the Internet, it can disappear even faster. One organization, created on the Internet, offered to attach its mark "TRUSTe" to businesses as a sign of trustworthiness.[51] It is of questionable success because some businesses that carried the sign did not live up to the reasonable expectations of the consumers. Consumers reached the conclusion that TRUSTe did not sufficiently monitor, enforce, or inform about, the promises of its sign.[52]

Internet businesses have piggy-backed on trusted real space businesses because customers seem to trust businesses in real space more than they do businesses in cyberspace. For example, community banks with a loyal customer-base can establish similar relationships on the Internet, and far larger financial institutions may desire to link their products to such banks. Sometimes brick and mortar enterprises that have the loyalty and trust of their customers become aligned with Internet enterprises to bestow on those Internet enterprises the trust of the retailers' customers.

This arrangement is similar to franchising, franchising not of expertise or quality of goods, but of trust. For a similar reason, the value of real space brand names has risen on the Internet. Perhaps this may be one reason why trademark owners are so concerned about their trademarks and well-known brand names have acquired special protection by Congress.

III. THE ROLE OF LAW IN SUPPORT OF TRUSTING

Under certain circumstances, the reliability of trusted persons, institutions and other intermediaries cannot be fully supported

---

50   *See Center for Democracy and Technology,* https://www.cdt.org (last visited Aug. 15, 2023) (at one time seeking "practical solutions to enhance free expression and privacy in global communication technologies").

51   *See TRUSTe, formerly at* http://www.truste.org (committed to helping web users "protect themselves online").

52   Groups with similar interests undertake to enforce the members' obligations to be trustworthy, thereby maintaining the trustworthiness of the group. *See* Tamar Frankel, *Should Funds and Investment Advisers Establish a Self-regulatory Organization?, in* THE FINANCIAL SERVICES REVOLUTION, UNDERSTANDING THE CHANGING ROLES OF BANKS, MUTUAL FUNDS AND INSURANCE COMPANIES, 447, 451 (Clifford E. Kirsch ed., 1997) (explaining that membership organizations protect the members' reputations while also establishing ethical standards).

by the trusted parties themselves. There comes a point when the parties will not interact because their costs of verification and proof of trustworthiness will exceed their joint benefits from the transaction. In these circumstances, legal backing is necessary.[53] Law offers benefits to both parties. It offers trusting people reduced risks by preventive regulation of institutions and intermediaries, before the fact, and compensation as well as punishing violators, after the fact. Law offers trusted persons a "brand name" guarantee of their trustworthiness, which may be too costly for trusted persons to create or buy in the markets. These supports for trusting are financed not by private sector interested persons, but by all taxpayers. Hence, the cost of maintaining a trusting system as a whole, in addition to the users of trust relationships, is subsidized and distributed among a large group through government intermediation. Further, law strengthens norms of behavior, and reduces the cost of enforcement. People become trustworthy through habit, with a lower threat of punishment.

Trust verification, especially verification by third parties, is layered. The first layer is composed of direct trusting relationships. The second layer, in lieu of or in addition to personal trust, consists of market verifiers. The third layer is composed of verifying the verifiers-the law. Law regulates trusted persons and intermediaries as well as market verifiers, who establish the trustworthiness of others.

The law can regulate intermediaries more effectively than individuals. Intermediaries are often less mobile than individuals and their number is smaller. As the size of private sector actors and intermediaries increases, they are likely to be the first-tier

---

53   For example, assume that a person wishes to hand over his life's savings, $100, to a manager, expecting $7 in additional benefits in terms of performance and free time, and paying the manager $1 for his work. Assume further that the probability of losing the $100 through the manager's conversion or incompetence is 50%. The person will not engage in this transaction because he will not risk losing $50 even if the probability of gaining $6 is very high. He will, however, interact if the manager provides him with assurance as to the integrity of the money. However, the manager cannot expend more than $1 minus his living expenses to provide that assurance. If the cost to the manager of assuring his trustworthiness is higher, he will not offer it and the parties will not interact. Someone will have to bridge the gap. That someone may be market verifiers, who can offer verification at a reduced rate, or the law, through a requirement for insurance, examinations, and other preventive measures, can ensure either that the money will not be converted, or that the manager is competent. Trusted private sector qualifiers, however, must also prove their trustworthiness. The law regulates the most trusted private sector qualifiers, such as lawyers and accountants.

gatekeepers and enforcers of the law within their operational territories, including international enforcement. Mergers of banks and businesses are usually accompanied by stricter requirements for self-regulation, controls of illegal acts within the organizations, and trustworthiness towards customers. Professional private sector gatekeepers, such as accountants, are subject to increasingly strict regulation as they testify to the trustworthiness of businesses in real space and on the Internet. In contrast, individuals' costs of establishing the trustworthiness of institutions and other specialized intermediaries are very high. Even though their number is small, they are composed of many individuals and their internal activities are not open to individual customers. More importantly, individuals cannot adopt preventive measures to ensure the intermediaries' trustworthiness even though the risks that individuals take, in entrusting their property to institutions, may be very high.

As the importance of the role of intermediaries increases on the Internet, the importance of law in reducing the customers' risks and increasing the trustworthiness of the intermediaries increases. In reaction to consumers' concerns and Congressional prodding, industries began to establish best practices in respect to privacy issues. While customers may rely on some industries' best practices, for financial intermediaries, best practices were held insufficient. The danger of losing public trust is too great and the consequences too grave. Further, the law is most important when the public voices its concern on particular issues.

On the Internet, financial intermediaries need a higher degree of public trust, as they are eager to cut their costs by establishing Internet communications with customers. Hence, Congress directed regulators to impose rules of confidentiality on financial intermediaries.[54] On March 2, 2000, the Securities and Exchange Commission published a proposed rule that would restrict broker dealers', investment companies', and registered investment advisers' ability to utilize customers' personal nonpublic information.[55] Bank regulators are proposing similar rules.[56]

---

54   *See* Gramm-Leach-Bliley Act §504, 15 U.S.C. §6804 (requiring specified federal agencies to adopt rules restricting the ability of certain financial institutions to "disclose nonpublic personal information about consumers").

55   *See* Privacy of Consumer Financial Information (Regulation S-P), 65 Fed. Reg. 12,354 (2000), 17 C.F.R. pt. 248 (proposed Mar. 2, 2000), expanded to other financial institutions in 12 C.F.R. §1016 *et seq.*

56   *See* Privacy of Consumer Financial Information, 65 Fed. Reg. 8770 (2000), 12 C.F.R. pt. 332 (proposed Feb. 22, 2000).

The Internet has both increased and decreased the cost of law enforcement. It is unclear what the net costs are. The increased costs are caused by the global impact of the Internet beyond state boundaries. The decrease is based mainly on ease of communication, such as consumers' complaints, information from other agencies and other countries, and technical innovations, such as surfing the Internet for fraudulent advertising.

The Internet and the law affect each other. For example, the contract rule of *caveat emptor* is sufficient to create trusting among buyers and sellers in face to-face relationships, but not in e-mail communications. Hence, contract doctrine may change and become more "fiduciary-like" and customer friendly. The requirement to tell the truth and be reliable will not be linked to the parties' explicit agreements, but to the default rules that underlie fiduciary law or to stronger fairness concepts in contract law. These may creep into, and create, the "contract law of the Internet." Not only will these rules reflect best practices of industries doing business on the Internet, but also they will be recognized as crucial to the development of e-business, and as such, acquire the power and weight sufficient to change legal doctrine.

IV. THE ROLE OF TECHNOLOGY IN SUPPORT OF TRUSTING

Technology has helped reduce customers' risks by eliminating the need to send card account information over the Internet. While the solution is not yet certain, it seems clear that the issue must be resolved if consumers are to consider the Internet as their main form of communication with businesses.

In some situations, enforcing the law against violations on the Internet may be as easy, or even easier, than enforcing the law in real space. In recognition that "code is law," as Professor Lawrence Lessig argues, government may regulate certain aspects of Internet operations through code-the means of Internet communication.[57] It is likely that the government will use this method to fight against serious crimes, which the Internet greatly facilitates. This method raises issues of government accountability, which are beyond the scope of this paper. But technology and protection can prompt

---

[57] *See* Lawrence Lessig, CODE AND OTHER LAWS OF CYBERSPACE (1999); Lawrence Lessig, *Preface to Trust,* 81 B.U.L. REV. 329 (2001) (stating that the use of code or technology can obviate the need to trust).

distrust and eliminate some trusting behavior, as Professors Lessig and Helen Nissenbaum note.[58]

The solutions devised to date are operational, technological, and organizational. On the operational and organizational side, experts suggest that consumers avoid some forms of payment on the Internet, such as debit cards. These cards resemble cash and are too risky. Processes, such as the process by which credit cards are settled, may have to change. Credit card transactions that follow real world processes, from merchant to a merchant processor and then to a credit card association, expose the parties to risks from thieves. Among others, a safer approach is to let the merchant directly query the credit card issuing bank for payment authorization. Non face-to-face merchants are required to take an additional step when they authorize a purchase. Businesses are using different payment systems for online shopping, such as digital certificates. There are digital identity services and technical forms of authentication that help reduce consumers' risk. Non-technical solutions are also recommended, such as the use of employees for internal controls, response to possible threats and risks, and the hiring of experts.

On the technological side, businesses are adopting protections against third party attacks on the Internet business by technical solutions. These include anti-spamming software and filters against "denial of service attacks." Most companies have installed secure sockets layer mechanisms to protect web transactions. Businesses injured by harmful misinformation that frightens customers away, use trusted sources to combat these harmful effects. The important point is that corrections come from a trusted source. And, of course, some businesses choose not to disclose the problems they have, but to simply correct them.

V. CONCLUSION

In real space and on the Internet, trust and non-trust pose the same issues. The ways people come to trust in real space and cyberspace differ, however. That is mainly because the benefits, costs, and risks in Internet interaction have changed and have been reallocated among sellers and buyers. The costs have shifted

---

58 *See id.* (arguing that technological protection replaces the important social act of trusting). *See also* Helen Nissenbaum, *Securing Trust Online: Wisdom or Oxymoron?* 81 B.U.L. REV. 101 (2001) (arguing that security measures on the internet actually lower trusting behaviors by creating safe environments under which the act of trusting, *i.e.,* the act of being vulnerable to another's discretion, is unnecessary).

to sellers in order to achieve the same goal-establishing trusting relationships on which economic activity depends.

The model that emerges is that of "layered trusting supports." No one layer can create a culture of trust. Reputable institutions and intermediaries, verifiers, and providers of trust services, contribute to public trusting. But more of them are needed on the Internet, and the law must continue to provide the backbone of legitimacy for their trustworthiness. Perhaps stronger support is needed on certain issues. For example, the Internet offers grand scale opportunities to destroy software in which communications and ideas are stored. To prevent such destruction, we may need a worldwide meta-norm. Today, destructive hackers are still considered the "smart kids" who playfully show off their genius. Against such damaging games, there is no strong norm that brings a general revulsion. If children were told, with their first computer, that computers are for creating, not for destroying; if children develop this attitude the way they develop the inhibition on playing with matches to avoid destruction, yet recognizing that fire is good, as the parents show by lighting candles and the fireplace, then over time a meta-norm can rise to be enforced not only by governments, but also by members of the public. As the meta norm becomes stronger, law's interference can become weaker. But this is a goal for the future. We can begin by using the tools, based on the elements of benefits, costs, and risks, and adjusting them to the new Internet environment.

THE INTERNET, SECURITIES REGULATION, AND THEORY OF LAW

THE INTERNET, SECURITIES REGULATION, AND THEORY OF LAW*

Tamar Frankel

INTRODUCTION

Rarely has a change in the environment affected society as dramatically as the Internet. It has transformed the way we retain, transfer, and exchange information. At minimal cost, the Internet offers far more information at a faster pace than ever before. It enables us to interact around the globe with more people than at any time in the past. When such dramatic environmental changes occur, drastic changes in the law often follow.[1]

*   Tamar Frankel, *The Internet, Securities Regulation, and Theory of Law* was previously published at 73 CHI.-KENT. L. REV. 1319. Copyright (c) 1998 Chicago-Kent College of Law. Reprinted with permission. *Available for download* https://scholarship.kentlaw.iit.edu/cklawreview/vol73/iss4/14.

I am indebted to Professors Hugh Baxter and Wendy Gordon of Boston University School of Law for their insightful comments on this article. Many thanks to my assistants Dan Pierce and William Hecker for their meticulous research and editorial comments.

1   Professors Monroe E. Price and John F. Duffy have explained that "judges and legislators frequently invoke technological change as a justification for altering regulatory arrangements, revising statutes, or reconsidering constitutional doctrine." Monroe E. Price & John F. Duffy, *Technological Change and Doctrinal Persistence: Telecommunications Reform in Congress and the Court,* 97 COLUM. L. REV. 976, 976 (1997). They posit that this may be especially so when the technological change affects instruments of speech. *See id.* at 977. *See generally* Michael A. Geist, *The Reality of Bytes: Regulating Economic Activity in the Age of the Internet,* 73 WASH. L. REV. 521 (1998) (discussing the development of Internet law, the impact of the Internet on economic regulation, and proposals for adapting economic regulation to the Internet, suggesting that no single approach is adequate).

The Internet affects the environment in which securities markets operate and the laws that govern them.[2] The use of the Internet has already begun to change the way information about securities is disseminated and the way securities are traded,[3] two activities regulated by the securities laws.[4]

The purpose of this article is to begin an inquiry on a number of questions: Should the securities laws be adapted to the use of the Internet? If so, how? What path of inquiry should be taken to answer the questions, and how should we think about adapting law to a changing environment of actors and actions subject to

2   *See, e.g.*, Donald C. Langevoort, *Information Technology and the Structure of Securities Regulation,* 98 Harv. L. Rev. 747, 748 (1985) ("Technology also affects the securities market on a more fundamental level: it alters the market's structure."). Like it has securities laws, the Internet has changed the regime in which many types of commercial transactions occur. For a discussion of some of these changes, *see* Diana J.P. McKenzie, *Commerce on the Net: Surfing Through Cyberspace Without Getting Wet,* 14 J. Marshall J. Computer & Info. L. 247 (1996) (attempting to identify some areas of potential liability for persons conducting business in cyberspace). At the beginning of 1999, SEC Chairman Arthur Levitt expressed his concern at the impact that Internet trading has had on the patterns of investors' behavior. He noticed a 330 percent increase in investor complaints concerning Internet trading. The very speed and ease of placing trades on-line encouraged certain patterns of behavior that exposed investors to higher risks. Chairman Levitt warned investors against such tendencies. He has not suggested, however, any imminent changes in the rules. *See* SEC Chairman Levitt Addresses Internet Trading Concerns, Fed. Sec. L. Rep. CCH No. 1859, *at* 1 (Feb. 3, 1999).

3   The Internet and other methods of electronic media have created major environmental changes in areas other than securities regulation. *See, e.g.*, Mark E. Budnitz, *Stored Value Cards and the Consumer: The Need for Regulation,* 46 Am. U.L. Rev. 1027 (1997) (arguing that federal legislation is needed in the area of electronic cash to ensure the integrity of the payment system because many consumers are confused about the nature of the arising system). Professor Budnitz' examination of electronic cash perhaps provides a good analogy to the situation regarding securities regulation. Like the regime he described, the integrity of the securities markets may be threatened by the emergence of the Internet if its use is not properly regulated. I argue, however, that this is best done through the Commission and not through federal legislation.

4   For a discussion of another area where changes in technology have affected the securities markets and laws, *see* Charles W. Mooney, Jr., *Property, Credit, and Regulation Meet Information Technology: Clearance and Settlement in the Securities Markets,* 55 Law & Contemp. Probs. 131 (1992) (examining technology and commercial law in the context of securities market clearing and settlement). *See also Note, The Application of Securities Laws in Cyberspace: Jurisdictional and Regulatory Problems Posed by Internet Securities Transactions,* 18 Hastings Comm. & Ent. L.J. 901 (1996) (examining new securities law issues raised by the Internet).

law? These questions are limited to the securities acts regulating securities markets. The inquiry, however, is broader. It touches on the way law should change generally in a broader context of legal theory. The article starts by defining law, then examines two particular situations in which securities markets have used the Internet, and the lawmakers' response to these uses. The article concludes with a critical analysis of this response in the context of legal theory.

Part I of this article proposes a view of law as an adaptive, self-replicating system of coercive communications, consisting of three parts: substance of coercive communications, mechanisms for enforcement, and mechanisms and methods for changing law. Parts II and III of the article show how the three parts of the legal system react to behavioral changes of those who are regulated by law as their environment changes.

To examine the response of law in such cases, I chose two situations under the securities acts. The first, discussed in Part II of the article, deals with the use of the Internet to deliver prospectuses. The Securities and Exchange Commission ("Commission") issued an interpretive release in connection with transfers by the Internet in a way that maintained the status quo.[5] In this manner, the Commission allowed issuers and some investors to capture the benefits of the Internet, while reducing adverse effects of this use on other investors, in furtherance of the policies of the securities acts.[6] The three-part model of law is applied to analyze the adaptation of the securities laws on this subject.

Part III of the article describes the regulation of securities exchanges—a species of securities trading markets—and the use of the Internet to establish on-line trading sites. In some cases, the staff of the Commission allowed issuers to provide such trading sites to their shareholders.[7] Applying the model of law to this example, the far-reaching implications of such permission are highlighted and lead to a proposed method of adapting the securities laws to Internet trading sites.

5   See Use of Electronic Media for Delivery Purposes, Securities Act Release No. 7233, 60 Fed. Reg. 53,458, 53,459 (Oct. 13, 1995) (noting that release does not affect parties' rights or responsibilities under the securities laws).

6   See id. at 53,458 (noting benefits of electronic distribution).

7   See, e.g., Real Goods Trading Corp., SEC No-Action Letter, (1996-1997 Transfer Binder) Fed. Sec. L. Rep. CCH ¶77,226, at 77,131 (June 24, 1996).

Here, we must reexamine fundamental policies underlying the law and adopt a new format of changing and enforcing law. This Part examines an emerging cooperative effort among the adaptive mechanisms of law: the Commission and custom-creating markets. I believe that in order to cope with the fundamental changes that the Internet may introduce into the securities markets, two parts of law's adaptive structure—the Commission and the markets—must closely interact to allow for experiments and controls almost simultaneously. These two actors are already moving in this direction.

The proposed three-part model of law is designed to provide a framework for explaining, and especially guiding, the way we think about adapting law to changes in the environment of actors. Hopefully, a developed model will help predict the law's response to changes in the environment. Technology and markets are not the only drivers of legal change; law is also affected by the existing legal infrastructure, which may provide actors both incentives and disincentives to certain behavior and changed environments. The focus of this article, however, is on adaptation of law to changes in people's behavior as their environment changes.

The inquiry here transcends the particular issues under the securities laws. It may help develop a broader generalization—a model of law's adaptation to the changed environments of those whom it regulates. As we are experiencing an ever-increasing pace of change in all aspects of our lives, a systematic inquiry into the response of law to change is critical.

I. A View of Law: A Three-part Adaptive, Self-replicating System of Coercive Communications Used to Help Organize Society

I view law as an adaptive, self-replicating system of coercive communications.[8] While not the only view of law, this view provides a useful framework for examining law's response to a changing environment. "Changing environment" means changing beliefs, activities, and behavior of actors in the society. "Response of law" means response to this changing environment—changes in the

---

8   See Hugh Baxter, *Autopoiesis and the "Relative Autonomy" of Law*, 19 Cardozo L. Rev. 1987, 2037-39 (1998) (describing view that legal system is structurally coupled to societal system).

organizational rules under which society functions.[9] Further, there is no consensus on the concept of coercion. Some would view the law as coercive only if it is backed by the force of a political unit, such as the state.[10] I take a more expansive view of coercion to include the coercive force of custom. This, of course, means that there is no clear dividing line between law and social rules that people may feel constrained to follow without threat of state-enforced sanctions. We may distinguish between customary law that is sanctioned by "legal-like" sanctions and methods, and law that is not. In any event, the problem is not unique to our context here. The law concerning the definition of contracts as opposed to non-contract obligations poses similar issues and can provide a guide to the distinction as well.[11]

Law is a structured system. The structure consists of substance, enforcement mechanisms, and mechanisms and methods of adaptation. The term "system" denotes a holistic view of a complex arrangement composed of types of items and individual items related in a predictable pattern—a repetitious rhythm.[12] "Structure" denotes a stable relationship among the parts of the system: "The mutual relation of the constituent parts or elements

---

9   I do not view law as a living organism. It is a species of communication among actors in society. This communication helps organize society and its members' relationships and activities.

10   *See* John Austin, THE PROVINCE OF JURISPRUDENCE DETERMINED AND THE USES OF THE STUDY OF JURISPRUDENCE 13-23 (Noonday Press 1954) (1832, 1863) (defining "command" as idea that is sanctioned if disobeyed).

11   *See* 1 E. Allan Farnsworth, FARNSWORTH ON CONTRACTS 1.1, *at* 4 (2d ed. 1990) (defining "contract" as "a promise, or a set of promises, that the law will enforce or . . . recognize"; "(a) promise for which the promisee has given nothing in return" is generally not enforceable), now FARNSWORTH ON CONTRACTS (4th ed. 2019), updated by Zachary Wolfe.

12   A system is:
An organized or connected group of objects.
. . . . A set or assemblage of things connected, associated, or interdependent, so as to form a complex unity; a whole composed of parts in orderly arrangement according to some scheme or plan; rarely applied to a simple or small assemblage of things (nearly = "group" or "set").
[in linguistics:] A group of terms, units, or categories, in a paradigmatic relationship to one another.
17 THE OXFORD ENGLISH DICTIONARY 496 (2d ed. 1989). Thus, the term "system" focuses on the whole rather than its parts and on a pattern of relationships among the parts. In this sense, a system is predictable. However, a system need not be stable. For example, a system can be chaotic, so long as its parts consistently relate to each other in a chaotic manner.

of a whole as determining its peculiar nature or character . . . ."[13] The securities laws, with which I deal later, also constitute a system. We have a seamless web of systems within systems, from the atoms to the cosmos, each with somewhat different fundamental rules and yet each relating to the whole and to each other. Our organization of chaos into patterns of orders and systems is not a reality but one which we need in order to be able to think about issues and sort out solutions. This article deals with a specific legal system—the securities laws—and relates it to law generally, a broader system to which the securities laws belong.

A. Law Is a Structured System[14]

Law's structure contains three main parts: (1) the substance of coercive communications to members of a society; (2) mechanisms and methods of enforcing these communications; and (3) mechanisms and methods for adapting the structure and the substance of its components to changing environments.

The very act of enforcement can change law and many enforcement and adaptive mechanisms can perform both functions. Some mechanisms and their impact differ in degree. By enforcing the law, the police introduce some change, but not as much as legislatures or courts. It seems that the more "hands-on" enforcement mechanisms perform, the less immediate general impact they may have. Perhaps the police change law in a way similar to the way market actors change the law, gradually and

---

13   See 16 THE OXFORD ENGLISH DICTIONARY 959 (2d ed. 1989). See also id. ("an organized body or combination of mutually connected and dependent parts or elements," and "in a wider sense: (a) fabric or framework of material parts put together"). Thus, the earmarks of a structure are particular elements, and a relationship among them that is stable and paints the whole with the color of a unique identity. Arguably, a chaotic system does not have a structure because, although the relationship among its components gives the whole an identity, its structure is not sufficiently determinate.

14   The idea of this structure of law was triggered by Karl Popper's collection of lectures, The Myth of the Framework. See Karl R. Popper, *The Rationality of Scientific Revolutions: Selection Versus Instruction, in* THE MYTH OF THE FRAMEWORK 1 (M.A. Notturno ed., 1994). Popper compares and distinguishes three adaptive systems: genes, behavior, and scientific theories. See id. at 2-7. He says that all three adaptive systems have a current structure and each structure contains mechanisms for adapting to a changing environment in accordance with certain rules. See id. at 2-5. See also Hugh Baxter, *Autopoiesis and the "Relative Autonomy" of Law,* 19 CARDOZO L. REV. 1987, 2037-39 (1998) (describing that effect on communications by other systems depends on structures of legal system).

incrementally. Enforcement and change may be distinguished by their purpose, focus, and intended results. This distinction helps the analysis and justifies treating them separately.

1.   Substance

The main part of the law's structure consists of the substance of coercive communications to members of a society. This part is organized according to the generality of the communications: (1) specific decisions, defining the relationship among individuals and entities; (2) rules that apply generally to types of individuals and entities;[15] and (3) foundational norms, values, and policies that the rules are designed to implement.[16] Rules subsume and generalize specific decisions; values and policies subsume and generalize both latter types of items.[17] This format of

---

15   There are detailed statutes, rules, forms, and guidelines regarding the required disclosure for securities offerings, the prohibitions on offerings of unregistered securities, and the prohibitions on fraud. *See, e.g.,* 15 U.S.C. §77e(a) (prohibiting the sale of unregistered securities); *id.* §77aa (listing items of information required in a registration statement); *id.* §78j(b) (prohibiting fraud in connection with the purchase or sale of securities); 17 C.F.R. §§229.501-.502 (listing the items of information to appear in a prospectus). The rules governing the stock exchanges and behavior of broker-dealers provide for the orderly operation of the markets by prohibiting these intermediaries from taking unfair advantage of investors and issuers. *See* 15 U.S.C. §78f(b)(5) (stating that rules of an exchange "are designed to prevent fraudulent and manipulative acts and practices" and "to remove impediments to and perfect the mechanism of a free and open market and a national market system"); *id.* §78o-3(b)(6) (requiring similar objectives). These rules are promulgated by the exchanges and the National Association of Securities Dealers and reviewed by the Commission. *See id.* §78s (granting Commission oversight over self-regulatory organizations).

16   Underlying the securities laws are two paramount policies: the policy of protecting investors, designed to entice investors to put their money at risk in the markets, and the policy of facilitating capital formation, designed to assist issuers in raising capital. *See* H.R. Conf. Rep. No. 104-369, at 31 (1995), reprinted in 1995 U.S.C.C.A.N. 730, 730 (stating that the purpose of securities laws is "to protect investors and to maintain confidence in the securities markets" to benefit "national savings, capital formation, and investment"). These two objectives are considered beneficial to the public as a whole and to members of the public. *See, e.g.,* 15 U.S.C. §78n(a) (prohibiting solicitation of proxies in violation of the rules and regulations "as the Commission may prescribe as necessary or appropriate in the public interest or for the protection of investors"). They conflict to some extent and require a balancing, with a higher value given to protecting investors.

17   For example, the securities laws contain many decisions regarding wrongful fraudulent statements (or omissions) by a defendant to the detriment of a plaintiff. *See, e.g., In re MGSI Sec., Inc.,* Securities Act Release No. 7578

communication is not surprising. It mirrors the format in which humans retain information and is a usual format (though not the only one) of communicating, organizing, and retaining detailed and complex data.[18] To be sure, the features of legal substance are not as clear-cut. The characteristics of "legal values" can be attributable to non-legal disciplines as well.[19] However, taken together with law's other features there emerges a unique system that is distinguishable from other systems.

2.   Mechanisms and Methods of Enforcement

Law's structure contains mechanisms of enforcing law's communications. The mechanisms include designated actors that implement these coercive measures in law. The actors themselves are not part of law; their designation, however, is. Some measures are used by governments to enforce their coercive communications; others—usually similar mechanisms—are used by the public to enforce its customs. In addition, regulators and the courts recognize accepted customs and use their enforcement powers to coerce compliance with the dictates of these customs.[20] While law prescribes the identity of law enforcers and their methods,

(Sept. 10, 1998), *available in* LEXIS, Fedsec Library, Secrel File. These decisions may be based on Rule 10b-5 under the Securities Exchange Act of 1934, 17 C.F.R. §240.10b-5. The prohibitions on fraud, as many other securities acts' regulations, are based on two policies: protecting investors, to maintain their confidence in the markets' integrity, and the encouragement of capital formation. *See, e.g., Sargent v. Genesco, Inc.*, 492 F.2d 750, 760 (5th Cir. 1974) (stating that basic intent of the 1934 Act antifraud provisions is same as that of the 1934 Act: "to protect investors and instill confidence in the securities markets").

18   *Cf.* K. Eric Drexler, Engines of Creation 217-18 (1986) (pointing to the issue of information overload and the need for organizing information); Mary C. Potter, Remembering, *in* 3 Thinking: An Invitation to Cognitive Science 3, 4-17 (Daniel N. Osherson & Edward E. Smith eds., 1990) (describing process of encoding and retrieving information).

19   *See* Hugh Baxter, *Autopoiesis and the "Relative Autonomy" of Law*, 19 Cardozo L. Rev. 1987, 2037-62 (1998) (discussing view that legal system has "structural couplings" to other systems).

20   *See, e.g.,* U.C.C. §2-202(a) (1995) (final written expression may be explained or supplemented by course of dealing, usage of trade, or course of performance); John D. Calamari & Joseph M. Perillo, The Law of Contracts 3.13, *at* 155 (4th ed. 1998) (stating that course of performance, course of dealing, and trade usage are used in determining the intent of parties in interpreting a writing); W. Page Keeton et al., Prosser and Keeton on the Law of Torts 33, *at* 193-96 (W. Page Keeton ed., 5th ed. 1984) (discussing custom as evidence of the standard of reasonable conduct). *But see* Lisa Bernstein, *Merchant Law in a Merchant Court: Rethinking the Code's Search for Immanent Business Norms*, 144

enforcers, such as administrative agencies, can develop "soft" indirect enforcement mechanisms that produce compliance. These methods are effective when applied to regulated industries whose business depends on an ongoing relationship with regulators.[21]

3.   Mechanisms and Methods for Change

Mechanisms for change are part of an adaptive system and the structure of law. The existence of such mechanisms *per se* does not destabilize the structure; rather, the mechanisms are crucial to the continuous existence of the structure. The structure must be stable, as well as resilient to change. Without adaptability, the structure will be too brittle and break with even minor changes in the environment.

Adaptive mechanisms can cause changes in various parts of the structure, mostly in the number and sometimes nature of the individual items, of which the structure is the organizing pattern. Even if the types of items change, the structure may remain intact. However, the structure may lose its identity and become another type of system, or perish, if fundamental changes occur in the nature of the relationships among the items and types of items within the structure or in the main components of the structure.[22]

U. Pa. L. Rev. 1765 (1996) (critiquing the UCC's search for and application of "immanent business norms").

21   For example, rather than bring enforcement, administrative, or judicial proceedings, or together with such proceedings, administrative agencies can publish their opinions or concerns regarding certain practices that the regulators have observed emerging in the industry. The Commission's Division of Investment Management occasionally expresses its concerns in a letter to Matthew Fink, President of the Investment Company Institute, the trade association of the mutual fund industry. *See, e.g.*, Investment Co. Inst., 1993 SEC No-Act. LEXIS 673 (Apr. 19, 1993). Such publications and letters are relatively inexpensive and raise the industry's awareness and diligence. Similarly, regulators may seek information and education about the market practices from the industry and others. That allows regulators, industry, and consumers to develop a common language and mutual understanding. Arguably, regulators that come too close to industries can become captives of the industries. However, even if regulators become captive, captivity is partial because regulators are subject to congressional supervision and media surveillance. On the plus side, captivity of this sort encourages open discourse, effective enforcement measures, and avoidance of confrontational relationships that, in the last analysis, do not necessarily result in effective regulation.

22   This is the danger that is posed to the identity of legal systems from absorbing different definitions of relationship and abandoning some of the main features of law, such as coercion.

The same principles apply to law. Most adaptive changes in law do not affect the foundational components of law's structure nor the norms, values, policies, or types of items in the substantive part of the structure; they affect the content and the number of items in the parts of the structure, leaving the structure intact. However, if norms, values, or policies within the substance of law's coercive communications change in a fundamental way, or if the mechanisms for enforcement or mechanisms for change are eliminated or significantly altered, the particular legal system may be doomed to lose its identity; it may becme another kind of system or perish.[23]

In law, the mechanisms of change consist of four designated types of actors, each of which can create and adapt law: (1) legislatures that enact statutes or rules; (2) agencies that implement statutes, rules, and their own decisions, such as the Commission; (3) courts that adapt legislative statutes, rules, and their own decisions; and (4) markets that create and adapt customary laws.

Arguably, markets are part of the actors' environment rather than part of law. Clearly, markets are unique and distinguished from the three other lawmakers. First, in the markets, the actors that change the law and the actors that change the environment may be the same or closely connected. Business persons and lawyers create new customs or more likely adjust existing customs in reaction to an invention. Inventions that changed the environment and customary law are both products of the market. The Internet demonstrates this point.

Second, in market law, it is harder to identify the individuals or institutions that change law. To be sure, there are leaders that trigger a new or different path. Each follower leaves its imprint on and strengthens the coercive force of new customs. Moreover, the resulting customary laws can be attributed to preferences and decisions of a multitude of individuals. Thus, market customary laws are the product of actions and ideas of numerous individuals. Their hand may be visible, but not identifiable.

The difficulty of identifying the law changers has a number of benefits and disadvantages. On the minus side, among other things: (1) it is more difficult to attach responsibility to particular actors for changes in the law; (2) there is no requirement that the

---

23   For example, if law is shorn of its coercive component, it will cease to be law. If legal values are fully substituted by philosophical or economic values, law is likely to disappear and be subsumed in other disciplines.

changes will be rationalized or justified; (3) there are no review mechanisms regarding the substance of changed custom; (4) at the initial stage of change, it is difficult to predict where the change in customary law will lead and when it will end; and (5) market activities are difficult to monitor because few market actors have the duty to report.

Some of these disadvantages are reduced by the unique process of change: (1) review and legitimacy of an adaptive new custom depends on the degree of its following; (2) because custom must be publicized (or else it will have no followers), the rationalization of the changes in the custom may be aired in the public domain, similar to the public domain discussion of political ideas; (3) the itemized justification may not be as important when numerous actors follow the new custom. Their following is a "black box" that proves the custom's value, like the price of a product that determines its value, even though the buyers may have different reasons for buying the product; (4) market law does not become coercive immediately; law's coercive weight depends on the degree and intensity of its following. Thus, as adoption and following of market law—custom—grows, so does its coercive backing and its predictability. Hence, it is also less necessary to identify the persons who started breaking the new path; (5) whenever custom requires a review, amendment, or adoption, the other three mechanisms of change (the legislatures, courts, and administrative agencies) are available to perform the task; and (6) market activities and complaints about inadequacies of market law can be brought to the attention of the three other mechanisms of change by competitors, consumers, and other affected parties through hearings and by other means.

In addition, other lawmakers also change the environment in which law operates. The traditional lawmakers are increasingly drawing on the markets for the substance of law by incorporating "best practices" of industries.[24] Lawmakers also use the markets to enforce law through self-regulatory organizations, trade organizations, and other means.[25] Further, the Internet

24   *See* Governor Laurence H. Meyer, Address at Widener University (Apr. 16, 1998), *available at* https://www.federalreserve.gov/boarddocs/speeches/1998/199804162.htm (last visited Dec. 20, 2023), Banking Library, Fedpr File ("an important function of supervisors is to act as something of a clearinghouse for best practices.").

25   *See, e.g.,* 15 U.S.C. §78s (granting the Commission oversight authority over regulatory organizations); Investment Co. Inst., 1988 SEC No-Act. Lexis

environment is particularly conducive to the creation and enforcement of customary law. Many of the characteristics of customary law are immediately recognizable in the world of cyberspace. Markets have become a lawmaker in too many ways to be relegated to a mere environmental factor. Therefore, notwithstanding the differences between markets as lawmakers and other lawmakers, I consider markets to be lawmakers rather than the mere environment in which law operates.

Adaptive methods differ in different structures. Karl Popper has observed such differences in genetic, behavioral, and theoretical structures. In reaction to environmental changes, genetic systems mutate in a non-cognitive and non-intentional manner.[26] Those unlucky genes that do not mutate "correctly" die, and those lucky genes that happen to mutate in the "right" way live.[27] Behavioral systems usually adapt by intentional, cognitive actions using a trial and error method.[28] Unlucky actors that do not learn from the errors suffer the consequences and die, and those who tried the right way or learned from the errors live and prosper.

Scientific theories are changed cognitively as well, but unlike behavioral systems, changes are guided by reasoning (and partially by intuition).[29] The changes occur after rigorous testing by reasoning and experiments.[30] In addition, scientific theories must pass the testing of expert colleagues.[31] In some respects the process is similar to market adaptation. A leader breaks a new path and, unless he convinces the followers, the theory dies or lies dormant until such a following is formed. A similar

315 (Feb. 25, 1988) (noting that the Commission staff considered industry comments in its decision); Robert McGough, *Top Regulator Urges Industry to Reform*, WALL ST. J., Dec. 19, 1996, *at* C31 (noting that Barry Barbash, director of Commission Division of Investment Management, warned mutual fund industry about soft-dollar practices in recent speech).

26   *See* Karl R. Popper, *The Rationality of Scientific Revolutions: Selection Versus Instruction*, *in* THE MYTH OF THE FRAMEWORK 5 (M.A. Notturno ed., 1994) (noting that genetic mutations are not goal-directed).

27   *See id.* at 3 (noting that badly adapted mutations are eliminated).

28   *See id.* at 5 (noting that behavioral trials are goal-directed).

29   To some extent methods of law change, and changes in scientific theories are similar in that adaptations in scientific theories can also be distinguished by the methods chosen, *e.g.*, some scientists are theorizers, some are experimenters, and some choose to do both.

30   *Id.* at 6 (noting that scientific theories are open to investigation).

31   *See id.* at 7 (noting that scientific theories are open to criticism).

process applies to other lawmakers. The process, however, is more institutionalized, legitimizing change and its support only through the proper channels.

Adaptation of law is generally effected in three ways: (1) textual interpretation, by exploring meaning and applying analogy; (2) policy considerations, more remote from text: identifying the problem, explaining the problem, choosing the criteria for solutions, listing the options, and choosing the solutions in light of the criteria; and (3) culmination of decisions and actions of numerous individuals and units in the markets. However, all adaptation methods depend to a certain degree on followers and consensus, including desires of powerful organized groups. Adaptations are also affected by the lawmakers' own interests (e.g., to be re-elected or avoid being overruled by higher courts). These pressures rarely form part of the formal methods of adaptation; their existence, however, is recognized (and sometimes criticized).

Methods of adaptation depend to some extent on which type of lawmakers engage in adapting law. Custom adapts through a gradually increasing following.[32] The other three kinds of lawmakers—legislatures, courts, and administrative agencies—use methods similar to scientific theories' adaptations, based on cognitive decisions. However, courts and administrative agencies use both textual and policy methods, while legislatures use mostly policy methods.

Arguably, the methods of courts and administrative agencies differ: courts use a textual approach, while agencies use a policy analysis approach. I conclude, however, that both courts and agencies use both approaches. Administrative agencies must interpret the text of the governing legislation and follow its dictates to determine their authority and the guiding principles for

---

32   This method resembles in one respect the adaptation of genetic systems because it does not have a single cognitive intentional actor. *See id.* at 5 (noting that genetic mutations are not goal-directed). However, I do not view law as a living organism. Rather, I view it as a mechanism that society must have and develop in order to survive. Law is not the cell or the gene but rather the basic rules that enable the community to function, the analog of the rules that make the body and mind function. For example, living organisms develop a structure according to certain rules. The larger they are, the larger their bone structure must be. However, as societies become more complex, so does the law and other non-law rules that regulate the behavior of societies' members. I do not view law as a mere communication system because law is coercive. Mainly, these views, which are interesting and intriguing, are not useful for the inquiry undertaken in this article.

their actions. However, where agencies, such as the Commission, have powers that extend beyond judicial decisions, such as *ex ante* advisory powers or exemptive powers,[33] they may have to use a policy analysis approach. Some judicial decisions have taken the policy approach.[34]

B. Relation of Adapting Law to Existing Law

Karl Popper said that while all new scientific theories change at least parts of former theories, showing that the former theories are either wrong or incomplete, new theories encompass the (partial) truth of the theories they contradict.[35] Thus, Einstein's theory of relativity differs from Newton's theory by showing that

---

33 *See, e.g.*, 15 U.S.C. §80a-6(c) (authorizing the Commission to exempt parties or securities from the Investment Company Act of 1940 where in the public interest).

34 *See, e.g.*, *SEC v. Variable Annuity Life Ins. Co. of Am.*, 359 U.S. 65 (1959). In the VALIC case, the Supreme Court was asked to determine the law applicable to variable annuities. *See id.* at 66-69. This issue required classification of the annuities as either insurance or securities. The annuities had features of securities because the annuity contract holders, rather than the insurance company (as is the case with traditional fixed annuities), bore the risks and took the benefits of investment of the reserves funding these annuities. *See id.* at 70-71.

Justice Douglas, for the majority, adopted a doctrinal analysis, phrasing the issue in terms of a definition: Are variable annuities securities or are they insurance? *See id.* at 68. Justice Brennan took a policy approach: Do investors in variable annuities need the protection of the securities acts? *See id.* at 76 (Brennan, J., concurring). Justice Brennan concluded that variable annuities are both insurance and securities and that their classification would not be helpful to provide the answer. *See id.* at 80-81 (Brennan, J., concurring). Rather, his question led to the answer that, while in a traditional annuity the insurance company was a debtor that took the investment risk, in the new type of variable annuities the insurance company became a manager of other people's money, at their risk. *See id.* at 80 (Brennan, J., concurring). *See also id.* at 78 (Brennan, J., concurring) ("The situation changes where the coin of the company's obligation is not money but is rather the present condition of its investment portfolio. To this extent, the historic functions of state insurance regulation become meaningless." Hence, investors/annuity contract holders needed the protection of the securities acts.).

35 *See* Karl R. Popper, *The Rationality of Scientific Revolutions: Selection Versus Instruction, in* The Myth of the Framework 12 (M.A. Notturno ed., 1994) (noting that a new theory must be able to explain the success of the former theory, thus the former theory "must appear as a good approximation to the new theory").

it is not true in certain environments, yet subsumes Newton's theory for the limited environment as to which it is true.[36]

In law, the relationships between new and traditional policies and rules seem different than in science. Law can be tested by norms of right and wrong as well as by truth and falsity. Theoretically, norm setting seems to allow lawmakers more discretion to change existing laws than scientific theorizers would have; lawmakers can introduce new fundamental policies and values that fully trump and deviate from their predecessors rather than subsume them.

Yet, in reality, the way in which the law changes is astoundingly similar to the way in which new theories in science are fashioned.[37] Most new legal rules and underlying policies conflict with parts of their predecessors but contain and reaffirm part of their predecessors.[38] Generally, like most new scientific theories, new adaptive laws subsume most of prior laws and only "tweak" them in certain areas.

There can be a number of reasons for the conservative attitude of lawmakers to adapting and modifying law. In fact, these reasons are similar (and some are identical) to the reasons for the doctrine of *stare decisis*.

First, new laws are risky and costly for lawmakers and the regulated. Existing laws have been tested, and their strengths and weaknesses in a normally changing environment are known. New laws that have not been tested may bring unanticipated results.[39]

---

36 *See id.* at 21 (noting that Einstein's theory contains Newton's theory as an approximation); *id.* at 20 (noting that the old theory is "approximately valid for velocities which are small compared with the velocity of light").

37 Arguably, the problem lies not on our following the trodden paths but in not sufficiently breaking away from them. *See* K. Eric Drexler, Engines of Creation 461 (1986) ("The difficulty lies, not in the new ideas, but in escaping the old ones . . . ." (quoting John Maynard Keynes)).

38 *See, e.g., Basic Inc. v. Levinson*, 485 U.S. 224, 244 n.22 (1988) (noting that actions under Rule 10b-5 of the 1934 Act "are distinct from common-law deceit and misrepresentation claims, and are in part designed to add to the protections provided investors by the common law" (citations omitted)).

39 *See, e.g.*, Payment of Asset-Based Sales Loads by Registered Open-End Management Investment Companies, Investment Company Act Release No. 16,431, 53 Fed. Reg. 23,258, 23,264 (June 21, 1988) (noting that the use of Rule 12b-1 by the mutual fund industry "has resulted in many distribution practices that could not have been anticipated when the rule was adopted").

Unlike scientific theories,[40] it is almost impossible to test new laws in advance and limit these results.[41]

Second, new laws impose learning costs on the legal profession, lawmakers, the regulated, and the public. Even something as minor as the introduction of new section numbers to a body of law imposes such costs.[42] In addition, while old laws have been examined and interpreted, new laws must acquire their interpretative gloss. Developing this gloss is costly.

Third, we have a limited capacity for attention. That is why we create habits that put ourselves on "automatic pilot." Doing so enables us to pay attention to new and unexpected (and, therefore, more risky) events. Old laws are habitually followed by most people (or habitually not followed by some people). That is why, while they are excited by new ideas, people cannot easily break old habits. New laws require law-abiding citizens to break old habits and create habits of compliance.[43] That is costly.

Therefore, even when logic may require a complete break from the past, experience builds on the past. People rarely adopt entirely new values and policies or rules that do not relate to existing legal and social structures and behavioral norms.[44]

Finally, laws are not enacted in a vacuum. They do not start with a clean slate but against the backdrop of the other existing laws. Fundamental changes in the structure of law affect these other laws and may require drastic changes of all existing laws addressing the same area or subject matter. That is costly. Consequently, when changes in the laws are necessary, the bulk of existing law is left intact.

---

40 Arguably, even scientific theories cannot be accurately tested because the very testing, in some environments, changes the results.

41 This is why we favor state laws, dual regulation, and market experimentation, even if they may bring some adverse results. The receptive attitude to requests for exemptions and no-action letters by the Commission is in part due to the desire for information about market experimentation. *See* 1 Tamar Frankel & Arthur B. Laby, THE REGULATION OF MONEY MANAGERS 144-1 to 1-184 (Ann Taylor Schwing, ed. 2023).

42 If new numbers are introduced merely for the sake of symmetry, the cost may exceed the benefit.

43 *Cf.* Ragnar Granit, THE PURPOSIVE BRAIN 128 (1980) (physiologically people need and, therefore recreate, a stable world).

44 That is why "legal transplants" take roots successfully when they are planted in a fertile ground of familiar laws, ideas, culture, and history. Otherwise, they usually shrivel and die.

C. *Relationship of Environmental Changes to Legal Change*

The impact of a changed environment on law is not uniform. The impact depends on which part of the law's structure the changed environment affects. If the effect is on specific cases or rules, the impact of the rules will change. Therefore, rules must be amended in order to maintain the status quo: the fundamental policies which the rules implement. If, however, the changed environment affects the fundamental policies and the values on which the legal system is based, when the old order that is subject to regulation is changed, when different actors, driven by different incentives take the place of the old actors, then a far more complex response by the law may be necessary.

A new environment may eliminate the problems that existing laws, regulating the old order, were designed to reduce or eliminate; it may raise new problems that existing laws do not address. A new environment can lead to different problem definitions and values underlying the definition. In such cases the underlying policies and perhaps the very structure of the laws must be reexamined.[45]

II. REGULATION OF PROSPECTUS DELIVERY

The emerging cyberspace is posing significant challenges to legal adaptation. In the securities area, cyberspace has a serious impact in two senses. First, it creates an entirely different mode of communication. The question here is: How should legal rules change to accommodate the new communication technology? If cyberspace does not alter our fundamental values, how should legal rules adapt and change in order to maintain our current

---

45 An analogy to the discussion of electronic currency law again seems appropriate here. Mr. Brian W. Smith and Mr. Ramsey J. Wilson argue that a proposal for the development of such law should be constrained by two premises:

> First, the law should not stifle or steer without reason future technological development. . . . Further, regulations that focus heavily on technological distinctions between payment systems would be unwise, because: (1) it is likely that such distinctions will become antiquated quickly in this fast-paced industry; and (2) such distinctions fail to consider the substance of the underlying relationship between the parties.

Brian W. Smith & Ramsey J. Wilson, *How Best to Guide the Evolution of Electronic Currency Law,* 46 AM. U.L. REV. 1105, 1127 (1997). It is important to remember that we are dealing with a rapidly evolving area of technology. The difficult goal, of course, is to regulate Internet use to the extent necessary to protect investors while not stifling developments which bring about net efficiencies.

values? What should the substance of our rules be in light of the changing environment for the actors in the securities markets?

Second, cyberspace allows communication at an unheard of speed. The issue here is: Which mechanism and method for legal change is more suited to respond quickly in this new environment, recognizing that some existing mechanisms and methods of legal adaptation simply cannot operate at such speed? Police using a horse and buggy cannot match nor catch a speeding car, let alone a plane.

Based on the framework developed in Part I, these two issues relate to the substance of the legal system and to the mechanisms and methods of change of the legal system.

This Part of the article inquires into the impact of the Internet on the delivery of prospectuses. The securities acts regulate disclosure concerning securities offerings in a number of ways. Some information is required, and some information is prohibited.[46] The discussion here relates only to the requirement of delivering a prospectus to potential investors in a public offering.[47]

There are two main policies underlying the securities acts. One is to maintain investors' confidence in the integrity of the markets mainly through disclosure: reducing investors' information costs and shifting these costs to the issuers and others, such as market intermediaries, for whom the costs are lower.[48] The second policy underlying the securities acts is somewhat subservient to the first but has become increasingly important in recent years. This policy is to reduce the costs of and encourage capital formation.[49] The Commission is sensitive to the costs imposed on issuers and intermediaries and is sympathetic to means of reducing the regulatory costs.[50]

---

46 *See, e.g.,* 15 U.S.C. §77h(d) (prohibiting untrue statements in a registration statement); *id.* §77aa (listing the items of information required in a registration statement).

47 *See id.* §77e(b)(2) (requiring prospectus delivery under the 1933 Act).

48 *See* SEC: Report to the Congress: The Impact of Recent Technological Advances on the Securities Markets, https://www.sec.gov/news/studies/techrp97.htm (last visited Dec. 20, 2023).

49 *See* H.R. Rep. No. 104-622, *at* 16 (1996), *reprinted in* 1996 U.S.C.C.A.N. 3877, 3878 (noting that a purpose of the 1996 legislation is the promotion of capital formation).

50 *Id.* (noting that a purpose of the 1996 legislation is the promotion of capital formation).

A. Need to Adapt Securities Regulation to Internet Communications: Impact of the Internet on the Environment of the Actors that Are Subject to the Securities Laws

As compared to traditional modes of information transfer, the Internet can reduce the cost of transmitting information for issuers, intermediaries, and some investors. Hence, these parties sought to deliver and receive prospectuses through the Internet, and they asked the Commission to clarify the status of this form of information delivery.[51]

B. The Commission's Response to the Internet Environment: Substance, Enforcement, Mechanisms for Change, and Methods of Change

1. Impact on the Substance of the Securities Laws

As a new mode of communication, the Internet does not affect the desirability of information transfer, nor does it impose a different institutional arrangement concerning delivery of prospectuses. The new mode of information transfer affects only the manner in which the information is transferred. Thus, the use of the Internet does not change the values underlying the fundamental policies on which our securities laws are based, the criteria of what is good—which law should either leave alone or support—and bad—which the law should restrict or prohibit altogether. Further, prospectus delivery by the Internet does not seem to affect the fundamental policies of the securities acts. If the status quo for investors remains the same, the underlying policies of the securities acts are not adversely affected by the use of the Internet to deliver prospectuses. In fact, by reducing the costs of capital formation, the securities laws' policies are advanced.

---

51 *See id.* at 53,460 (noting that the release is intended to provide guidance regarding electronic delivery). In 1995, the Commission issued a detailed release accompanied by questions and answers that guided the use of the Internet for delivering prospectuses. *See id.* at 53,458. The Commission recognized the increase in electronic prospectus delivery in its November 1998 release proposing prospectus delivery reforms. *See* The Regulation of Securities Offerings, Securities Act Release No. 7606A, 63 Fed. Reg. 67,174, 67,223 (Dec. 4, 1998) ("Electronic delivery of prospectuses is becoming more common."); *cf. id.* at 67,216 (noting that the proposed easing of restrictions on communications during the offering process "would enable issuers and market participants to take significantly greater advantage of the Internet and other electronic media to communicate and deliver information to investors").

To maintain the status quo, the rules must be changed. Investors' costs of receiving prospectuses through the Internet must be examined. First, not all investors have access to the Internet or wish to receive prospectuses through the Internet.[52] Some of those who do, however, prefer to receive information through this new medium.[53] Clearly, if investors can choose between the new mode of information transfer and the traditional one, they can evaluate their costs and make the decision accordingly. This is precisely the first condition that the Commission imposed on the use of the Internet for prospectus delivery.[54] However, once investors make the choice, they bear the burden of notifying the senders if they change their mind. After their initial choice has been made, the mode of information transfer remains the same until they change the choice.

This, however, is not all. Prospectuses are written in English.[55] Information transfer through the Internet involves an electronic language as well. Therefore, regardless of the investors' consent, the Commission requires that the electronic language used to transfer the prospectuses not be unduly complex or unavailable.[56]

Professor Lawrence Lessig suggested that the first question we should ask about the regulation of the Internet is: "Should this new space, cyberspace, be regulated by analogy to the regulation of other space, not quite cyber, or should we give up analogy and start anew?"[57] In the area of prospectus delivery, the Commission chose the path of regulation by analogy.[58] Under existing laws,

---

52   See Use of Electronic Media for Delivery Purposes, Securities Act Release No. 7233, 60 Fed. Reg. 53,461 (Oct. 13, 1995) ("Not all investors purchasing securities could be presumed to have the ability to access the final prospectus via an Internet Web site.") See also Interpretive Release (May 4, 2000), last reviewed (Mar. 26, 2008).

53   See Use of Electronic Media for Delivery Purposes, Securities Act Release No. 7233, 60 Fed. Reg. 53,461 (Oct. 13, 1995), supplemented in Interpretive Release (Mar. 26, 2008) (noting that investor consent, coupled with notice and access, may satisfy the delivery requirement).

54   See id.

55   See 17 C.F.R. §230.403(c) (requiring English language for a registration statement).

56   See Use of Electronic Media for Delivery Purposes, Securities Act Release No. 7233, 60 Fed. Reg. 53,460-61 (Oct. 13, 1995) (discussing access).

57   Lawrence Lessig, The Path of Cyberlaw, 104 YALE L.J. 1743, 1743 (1995).

58   See Use of Electronic Media for Delivery Purposes, Securities Act Release No. 7233, 60 Fed. Reg. 53,460 (Oct. 13, 1995) ("The Commission believes

there are a number of acceptable ways to deliver a prospectus, such as the mails or physical handing over.[59] These traditional delivery forms have proven highly reliable.[60] There is less certainty today that Internet delivery will be as reliable, and investors bear a greater risk that prospectuses will fail to reach them. Therefore, the Commission required that senders of prospectuses receive some indication of receipt: for example, that the receiver downloaded or copied the information, or actively responded in some other way to the information.[61]

In addition, materials sent by the Internet may be intercepted and changed before they reach the recipient.[62] The Commission imposed conditions on the senders to reduce the recipient's risks to this possibility, subject to a reasonableness standard.[63] Presumably, the Commission determined that by agreeing to receive prospectuses through the Internet the investors do not agree to bear this risk, except where reasonable precautions by the issuers are insufficient. Thus, so long as the costs to the

that the question of whether delivery through electronic media has been achieved is most easily examined by analogy to paper delivery procedures."), *supplemented in* Interpretive Release (May 4, 2000), last reviewed (Mar. 26, 2008).

59   *See* 15 U.S.C. §77e(b)(2) (requiring securities to be accompanied or preceded by a prospectus); Securities Act Concepts and Their Effects on Capital Formation, Securities Act Release No. 7314, 61 Fed. Reg. 40,044, 40,047 (July 31, 1996) (discussing the fulfillment of delivery requirements by actual and constructive delivery), *supplemented in* Interpretive Release (May 4, 2000), last reviewed (Mar. 26, 2008).

60   *See* Use of Electronic Media for Delivery Purposes, Securities Act Release No. 7233, 60 Fed. Reg. 53,458 (Oct. 13, 1995) (implying benefits of paper delivery in requiring electronic delivery to meet the same requirements), *supplemented in* Interpretive Release (May 4, 2000), last reviewed (Mar. 26, 2008).

61   *See* Use of Electronic Media for Delivery Purposes, Securities Act Release No. 7233 60 Fed. Reg. 53,461 (Oct. 13, 1995), *supplemented in* Interpretive Release (Mar. 26, 2008).

62   *See* Use of Electronic Media for Delivery Purposes, Securities Act Release No. 7233 60 Fed. Reg. 53,461 (Oct. 13, 1995), *supplemented in* Interpretive Release (Mar. 26, 2008). (requiring those providing information to "take the reasonable precautions to ensure the integrity and security of that information").

63   *See* Use of Electronic Media for Delivery Purposes, Securities Act Release No. 7233, 60 Fed. Reg. 53,461 (Oct. 13, 1995), *supplemented in* Interpretive Release (Mar. 26, 2008), and relying on SEC Issues Interpretive Release on Use of Electronic Media (effective May 4, 2000).

information sender of protecting recipients from these risks are not high, the sender is liable.

In sum, the Commission allowed the use of the Internet and at the same time imposed conditions that equate information transfer through the new medium with information transfer through the mails and other traditional media. The law was adapted to the changing environment of the Internet by allowing its use (and its advantages) while maintaining the values and policies underlying the securities laws. The Internet rules have the same impact as the pre-Internet rules.[64]

2.   Response of Securities Laws' Enforcement Mechanisms

The enforcement mechanisms of the requirement for prospectus delivery are affected by the Internet. Arguably, the real world has lost control over the Internet—the cyberspace and the virtual world it has created.[65] Hence, some proponents of this view say: cyberspace should be left alone.[66] I beg to differ.

To be sure, a number of the traditional enforcement mechanisms of this "real" world cannot be effectively applied to the virtual world because the costs of such enforcement have

---

64   For other examples of the Commission's adaptation of the law to the use of the Internet, *see* Regulation of Exchanges and Alternative Trading Systems, Exchange Act Release No. 40,760, 63 Fed. Reg. 70,844, 70,847 (Dec. 22, 1998) (final rules); Regulation of Exchanges and Alternative Trading Systems, Exchange Act Release No. 39,884, 63 Fed. Reg. 23,504 (Apr. 29, 1998) (Proposing Release); Regulation of Exchanges, Exchange Act Release No. 38,672, 62 Fed. Reg. 30,485 (June 4, 1997) (Concept Release); Cross-Border Tender Offers, Business Combinations and Rights Offerings, Securities Act Release No. 7611, 63 Fed. Reg. 69,136 (Dec. 15, 1998) (Proposing Release); Statement of the Commission Regarding Use of Internet Web Sites to Offer Securities, Solicit Securities Transactions or Advertise Investment Services Offshore, Securities Act Release No. 7606A, 63 Fed. Reg. 67,174 (Dec. 4, 1998) (Proposing Release); Statement of the Commission Regarding Use of Internet Web Sites to Offer Securities, Solicit Securities Transactions or Advertise Investment Services Offshore, Securities Act Release No. 7516, 63 Fed. Reg. 14,806 (Mar. 27, 1998) (Interpretation); Regulation of Takeovers and Security Holder Communications, Securities Act Release No. 7607, 63 Fed. Reg. 67,331 (Dec. 4, 1998) (Proposing Release).

65   *See* David R. Johnson & David Post, *Law and Borders—The Rise of Law in Cyberspace*, 48 Stan. L. Rev. 1367, 1370 (1996) (arguing that the rise of a cyberspace network is destroying the power of local governments to control its behavior).

66   *Cf. id.* at 1380 ("Assertion by any local jurisdiction of the right to set the rules applicable to the "domain name space' is an illegitimate extra-territorial power grab.").

greatly risen. For example, the Internet has increased the cost of enforcing the prohibition on misleading statements and offers of securities without registration because it is more difficult to identify and apprehend the senders and because senders can reach many parties.[67] However, the loss of control is not complete so long as some connections exist, as they must, between the real world and the virtual world of the Internet.

First and foremost are the actors. They may exist in the two worlds, but none of them occupies only the virtual world. Law applies to these actors and their actions. The Internet allows actors to do things they could not do before, in ways they could not do before, or in less time that was required before, but that is all. It may be harder to locate some actors than to locate others, but most can still be located and disciplined. In principle, those in the real world can control the virtual world.

However, in the virtual world, governments' ability to enforce some of their rules has weakened.[68] The "earthbound" actors, such as the telephone companies and other technical staff or the National Science Foundation, are not necessarily those who communicate. These conduits may be justified in rejecting responsibility for the substance of the information they transmit. Therefore, there may be a need to adopt new enforcement mechanisms and perhaps different norms to effectively regulate the virtual world.[69] Further, the focus of enforcement may change. For example, rather than regulate securities offerings on which some securities acts are based, it may be more effective to regulate securities purchases. That would bring into play the issuers' acceptance of payments rather than their communications, and the payment mechanisms that may be more identifiable and subject to regulation. In addition, the securities issuers may be regulated to require them to disseminate information more frequently and fully.

Second, new enforcement mechanisms may be created. For example, a possible enforcement avenue is to provide incentives for a new profession to police the communications or the

---

67 *See* Katrina Brooker, *The Scary Rise of Internet Stock Scams*, FORTUNE, Oct. 26, 1998, *at* 187 (noting that the Internet enables "crooks" to find large numbers of "potential victims" "quickly, cheaply, and anonymously").

68 *Cf.* Dipak K. Rastogi, *Living Without Borders in* Understanding Business Environments (2000).

69 *See* Lawrence Lessig, *The Zones of Cyberspace*, 48 STAN. L. REV. 1403, 1407 (1996).

communicators on the Internet. Cyberspace gatekeepers could be required to receive approvals from, and pay for, the monitoring of such professional actors, similar to those who must receive and pay for audited financial statements or legal opinions in order to make a public offering of securities. Such incentives to professionals are effective because the profession obtains a government monopoly and can make a good living. The cost to the gatekeepers must, of course, be evaluated, but competition among the new professionals may reduce their fees. These fees may be far lower than the losses incurred by investors short-term and by the markets long-term when prohibition of harmful practices is not strictly enforced by government.

Third, technology is now being developed to limit and control access to the Internet or access to particular audiences. For example, offers to sophisticated investors that need not be accompanied by an effective registration statement and a statutory prospectus can be made either by providing investors with special keys to the particular offering sites or by announcing that the offerings are not available to all readers.[70] Alternatively, cautionary language on offerings that certain regulatory systems do not apply to them may prove effective.[71]

Fourth, the costs of enforcing law may have changed. But not all costs have increased; the Internet has helped reduce some of the costs.[72] Thus, securities law enforcement has used the new technology; for example, the Commission has established areas on its Internet site where investors can inform the Commission about violations of the law and ask questions from the staff.[73]

---

70   See, e.g., IPONET, SEC No-Action Letter, (1996-1997 Transfer Binder) Fed. Sec. L. Rep. CCH ¶77,252, at 77,270 (July 26, 1996).

71   See Comment, Who Needs Wall Street? The Dilemma of Regulating Securities Trading in Cyberspace, 5 CommLaw Conspectus 305, 309-10 (1997) (noting the Pennsylvania regulations and NASAA proposals involving cautionary language).

72   See Joseph F. Cella III & John Reed Stark, SEC Enforcement and the Internet: Meeting the Challenge of the Next Millenium, A Program for the Eagle and the Internet, 52 Bus. Law. 815, 836 (1997) (noting that Internet "scam artists" usually must surface because they want investors to contact them).

73   See id. at 844-46 (noting the establishment of an Enforcement Complaint Center and educational initiatives, including initiatives on the Commission's website and in Internet forums). The Commission's website can be found at http://www.sec.gov/ and offers many features to users, including information about the Commission, investor assistance and a forum for complaints, a

The Commission has used the Internet to warn investors against certain promises that are "too good to be true" because "they are" and to caution investors against fraudulent practices.[74] The National Association of Securities Dealers ("NASD") has a statutory power and duty of regulating the broker-dealer community, subject to the supervision of the Commission.[75] Among its duties, the NASD supervises the advertising of its members.[76] Since many broker-dealers use the Internet to advertise, the NASD has been using software that scans the Internet automatically and picks certain words, such as "assure," "secure," "guarantee," "20 percent and more," and similar words that denote a promise of high return and low risk.[77] These advertisements are then evaluated by examiners.[78] In short, fire can sometimes be fought with fire.

3. The Choice of Adaptive Mechanisms and Method of Adaptation

In the case of prospectus delivery, the Commission is the legitimate traditional adaptive mechanism and there is no reason to substitute another mechanism for it. The Commission's relationship with the industry is ongoing, as issuers file their registration statements with the Commission. The response of the agency to developments was quite prompt. In early 1995, the Commission guided the industry by publishing an Interpretive Release with respect to the delivery of prospectuses through the Internet.[79] This adaptation of the law to the changed circumstances

---

database of EDGAR filings, a digest of recent SEC statements, and current SEC rulemaking information.

74 *See Comment, Who Needs Wall Street? The Dilemma of Regulating Securities Trading in Cyberspace*, 5 COMMLAW CONSPECTUS 305, 312 (1997) (noting the establishment of an "Investor Alerts" section on the Commission's web page).

75 *See* 15 U.S.C. §78s (granting the Commission oversight authority over self-regulatory organizations).

76 *See* FIFRA Rule 2210 *at* 4171 (regulating communications with the public).

77 *See* Katrina Brooker, *The Scary Rise of Internet Stock Scams*, FORTUNE, Oct. 26, 1998, *at* 198 (noting NASD's use of NetWatch software program).

78 *See NASD Will Employ Automation to Beef Up Its Internet Surveillance*, SAN DIEGO UNION TRIB., Feb. 13, 1998, *at* C5 (noting that the NetWatch indicators will "serve as guides for further investigation").

79 *See* Use of Electronic Media for Delivery Purposes, Securities Act Release No. 7233, 60 Fed. Reg. 53,458 (Oct. 13, 1995).

of the industry and the market actors seems to have worked smoothly and quite well.[80]

III. REGULATION OF SECURITIES EXCHANGES

A second change in the environment of securities markets and its actors is the introduction of trading sites. In this case, sponsors or issuers offer the holders of securities a meeting place where buyers and sellers of the securities may trade. The Securities Exchange Act of 1934 regulates the securities markets, including exchanges, where investors trade their shares.[81] Since markets in the United States are mainly conducted by market intermediaries—broker-dealers, market makers, underwriters, and other institutions that have joined the markets, such as subsidiaries of bank holding companies and insurance companies—the primary regulation of these marketplaces or market systems is performed by a self-regulatory organization of the intermediaries, subject to the oversight of the Commission.[82]

Based on the framework developed in Part I, this Part inquires into the lawmakers' reaction to this new format of trading and into the need for adaptation of the law's substance, enforcement, and change mechanisms and methods.

The policies underlying the regulation of the exchanges can be summarized as: (1) maintaining investor confidence in the markets (treating investors, especially small investors, fairly, and avoiding overreaching and conflict of interest treatment of investors by market intermediaries);[83] (2)maintaining efficient markets from which both issuers and investors benefit (orderly markets, assuring instantaneous or timely public price information, effective enforcement of trades);[84] and (3) reducing the costs of trading.[85]

---

80   *See* Beth Duncan, *Wallman Suggests SEC Should Be Open to Seminal, Not Incremental, Change,* 29 SEC. REG. & L. REP. (BNA) 993 (July 18, 1997) (noting that the initial response was "dismay at the lack of specific guidance," but ultimately issuers were pleased).

81   *See* Securities Exchange Act of 1934, 15 U.S.C. §§78a-78mm.

82   *See id.* §78s (granting the Commission oversight and authority over self-regulatory organizations).

83   *See, e.g., id.* §78f(b)(5) (providing that the rules of an exchange "are designed to prevent fraudulent and manipulative acts and practices").

84   *See id.* (providing that rules of an exchange are designed "to remove impediments to and perfect the mechanism of a free and open market").

85   *See id.* (implying policy of reducing costs of trading).

A. Need to Adapt Securities Regulation to Internet Communications: Impact of the Internet on the Environment of Actors that Maintain Exchanges and Trade on Exchanges

Because the Internet can be used to exchange information, it can be used as a forum for securities trading, similar to securities exchanges. Entrepreneurs, issuers, or market intermediaries (e.g., brokers and dealers) can set up websites, inviting shareholders for free or for a fee (or other form of compensation) to enter the sites and trade with other shareholders. For holders of shares that are not traded on exchanges and have illiquid or no markets, such websites are likely to increase liquidity. Shareholders value liquidity and are willing to forego returns on liquid shares. Therefore, for the issuers generally and issuers of illiquid securities especially, such trading sites can reduce the cost of capital.

Trading sites established by actors other than groups of intermediaries are a new phenomenon.[86] The current securities laws regulating exchanges do not fit these trading sites. The Commission was asked to determine whether trading websites fall within the definition of "exchange" in the Securities Exchange Act of 1934, whether they should be regulated, and if so, how. In response to a request for clarification of the status of trading sites, the staff issued several no-action letters that allow the opening of such sites under certain conditions.[87] This discussion is limited to sites established by issuers of securities, providing a forum for trading by the holders of their securities.

---

[86]   *See* Steven M.H. Wallman, *Regulating in a World of Technological and Global Change*, Metropolitan Corp. Couns. at 1 n.2 (Oct. 1996) ("Some companies have already set up Internet trading sites.").

[87]   A no-action letter was granted to Real Goods Trading Corporation ("RGTC") on June 24, 1996, allowing it to establish an "off the grid" trading system for its common stock. *See* Real Goods Trading Corp., SEC No-Action Letter, (1996-1997 Transfer Binder) Fed. Sec. L. Rep. CCH ¶77,226, *at* 77,131 (June 24, 1996). Since granting the no-action letter to RGTC, the Commission has granted such letters to other corporations proposing to operate similar sites and will no longer respond to such requests "unless they present novel or unusual issues." Flamemaster Corp., SEC No-Action Letter, 1996 WL 762990, at 6 (Oct. 29, 1996). The Commission has spoken only vaguely about other areas where the Internet may affect the secondary market. *See* SEC: Report to the Congress: The Impact of Recent Technological Advances on the Securities Markets, https://www.sec.gov/news/studies/techrp97.htm (last visited Dec. 20, 2023).

To evaluate the impact of the need for changing the securities laws, we first examine the impact of the Internet on the actors that maintain and trade on exchanges and trading sites by exploring the differences and similarities between trading sites and traditional exchanges. Internet trading sites and exchanges are similar in that they offer trading forums to investors and the benefit of liquidity.[88] However, this similarity is not as close as it seems at first blush because Internet trading sites offer a trading forum to investors who "do it themselves,"[89] while the exchanges are forums for intermediaries who trade on behalf of investors or to some extent for their own accounts.[90] Thus, both the promoters and users of the sites are different from those involved in exchanges.

In essence, trading sites eliminate the broker-dealers and other securities intermediaries, resulting in benefits and costs to investors.[91] On the benefits side, sites eliminate the cost of intermediaries and the risks from intermediaries' overreaching. However, Internet trading sites pose for investors a number of dangers—dangers against which they are protected by the intermediaries in traditional exchanges and other securities markets. When the intermediaries leave, these dangers appear.

88 Issuers who promote trading sites are interested in offering their shareholders an inexpensive trading forum to reduce the issuers' cost of capital.

89 RGTC did not propose to execute or settle transactions itself, but merely to provide a passive "bulletin board," which would provide information about prospective buyers and sellers of its stock. See Real Goods Trading Corp., SEC No-Action Letter, (1996-1997 Transfer Binder) Fed. Sec. L. Rep. CCH ¶77,226, at 77,131 (June 24, 1996). Any transactions would occur only through direct contact between participants who would need their own exemptions from the securities acts. See id. at 77,132. Presumably, these trades could be effectuated through broker-dealers or by eliminating the role of the broker-dealer, through the issuer's transfer agent, or by physically exchanging the paper shares.

90 See 15 U.S.C. §78c(a)(1) (defining "exchange"); id. §78k(a)(1) (prohibiting exchange members from trading on their own accounts, with exceptions).

91 Professor Donald Langevoort took an early view of the impact of information technology on the structure of securities regulation. See Donald C. Langevoort, Information Technology and the Structure of Securities Regulation, 98 HARV. L. REV. 747 (1985). He pointed out that the current regulatory structure assigns significant roles to intermediaries and argued that if regulators believe these roles are important, they must either "use the regulatory apparatus to maintain the intermediaries' position, and thereby impede generally beneficial market forces, or seek an alternative means to perform the functions." Id. at 764.

Intermediaries serve two crucial functions in the markets. First, they ensure that the parties will not renege on the trades.[92] More often than not, securities trades cannot be executed simultaneously.[93] Because securities markets are volatile, either sellers or buyers would usually have incentive to renege on the trades before execution.[94] If that happened often and investors learn about this risk, they would either demand high returns or cease trading; no markets would develop.

Intermediaries ensure the execution of trades by acting as escrow agents, holding both sellers' securities and buyers' money.[95] Since these intermediaries obtain their commissions upon execution of the trades, they have strong incentives to ensure the execution and bear the costs. If traditional intermediaries disappear and no mechanism fills the void, it is likely that trading-site markets will not continue to function, as investors find their trade agreements ineffective and too costly to enforce. Further, if investors do not understand the working of the markets, this experience may also reduce their trust in the traditional markets.

Second, intermediaries publish the prices of the trades.[96] Price information substantially reduces the trading costs for other investors because it offers shorthand information about the value

---

92   *See* 1 Tamar Frankel, SECURITIZATION: STRUCTURED FINANCING, FINANCIAL ASSETS POOLS, AND ASSET-BACKED SECURITIES 3.2.2.3, at 78 (2d ed., Ann Taylor Schwing, ed. 2005) ("Institutions rarely dishonor their obligations to lend or pay up their demand obligations, except when they fail.").

93   *See* Richard A. Booth, *The Uncertain Case for Regulating Program Trading*, 1994 COLUM. BUS. L. REV. 1, 61 (noting that "in a made market . . . buyers and sellers need not be simultaneously present for a trade to occur").

94   *See* 1 Tamar Frankel, SECURITIZATION: STRUCTURED FINANCING, FINANCIAL ASSETS POOLS, AND ASSET-BACKED SECURITIES 3.2.2.3, at 78 (2d ed., Ann Taylor Schwing, ed. 2005) ("Price fluctuations tempt buyers and sellers to breach their obligations when gains and losses are high.").

95   *See* 12 C.F.R. §220.4 (requiring intermediaries to receive securities price within one payment period, or sell the securities to pay for them); 17 C.F.R. §31.8(a)(1) (requiring leverage transaction merchants to maintain cover); *id.* §240.15c3-3(b) (requiring brokers or dealers to control securities subject to sale or vouch for availability).

96   *See id.* §240.11Ac1-1(b)(1) (requiring exchanges and associations to establish procedures for making bids available to exchange members); *id.* §240.11Ac1-1(c)(1) (requiring members to communicate bids and offers to exchange or association); Rule 60(b), 2 N.Y.S.E. Guide CCH ¶2060, at 2645 (Nov. 1996) (requiring members to comply with the Commission rule); Rule 60(c), *id.*, at 2645-46 (requiring exchanges to make bids and offers reported by specialists available to quotation vendors).

of the traded securities. The duty to publish the prices is not imposed on the parties to the trades but on those who service traders.[97] If these service providers disappear, someone else must provide the services as a condition to maintenance of efficient markets. Further, even though price information benefits investors generally, not all traders are interested in publishing the price of their bid or ask price.[98] Individual investors may wish to shield their offer or bid prices because this information may signal their trading position or give the wrong signal about their evaluation of the securities.[99]

Third, trading sites need not be connected to other trading exchanges. If they develop in isolation, and if different promoters offer sites for trades in the same securities, inefficient segmented markets may develop, with different prices for the same securities.

Fourth, issuers' control of trading sites poses unique threats to the integrity of the sites. Issuers may be tempted to affect the price of their securities.[100] Moreover, trading sites arguably pose a competitive threat to established exchanges if the sites provide the same services to investors at lower costs. Such competition may be unfair if trading sites remain unregulated while the exchanges bear regulatory costs. Although competition can enhance the efficiency of the exchanges, an unequal playing field can threaten

---

97   See 17 C.F.R. §240.11Ac1-1(b)(1), (c)(1); Rule 60(b)-(c), 2 N.Y.S.E. Guide CCH ¶2060, at 2645-46.

98   If an investor wishes to sell at a price and there are no buyers, he may wish to reduce his asking price, but not publish the reduction. There are mechanisms that would allow the lower price to be disclosed only to a buyer that agreed to buy at the higher price. Once that buyer commits to the purchase, the buyer may discover that he could get the stock at a lower price. On the other hand, if the asking price is not lowered, there may still be no buyers. The publication may, therefore, depend on the desires of the seller or the buyer, as the case may be.

99   The market in government securities provides a good example. There are few main dealers that are allowed to bid on government securities. See Business Briefs, N.Y. Post, Oct. 1, 1998, at 34 (noting that the Federal Reserve Bank of New York recognizes 33 primary government securities dealers). See also 5 C.F.R. §6801.102(f) (defining "primary government securities dealer" as "a firm with which the Federal Reserve conducts its open market operations"). They may trade among themselves. However, they would rather not inform each other of their need for either cash or securities. Hence, they long ago established a buffer, a broker who receives orders of buy and sell on condition of anonymity.

100 Higher prices indicate successful operations, help raise funds, facilitate planned mergers and acquisitions, and protect against takeovers. Lower prices can facilitate repurchase of company stock or management leveraged buyouts.

their existence in the future. Since the United States exchanges, especially the New York Stock Exchange, are among the most, if not the most, efficient exchanges in the world, the risk of their lost hegemony by action or inaction of the Commission can have serious consequences. Thus, before trading sites are allowed to proceed, the continued viability of the existing securities markets should be ensured, at least until it is clear that trading sites can provide a viable alternative to existing markets. At the same time, because I believe that competition *per se* is desirable as a matter of policy, attempts should be made to allow trading sites to develop under certain conditions.

In fact, the Commission has adopted a new regulatory framework to allow alternative electronic trading systems, as it attempts to adapt the law to the new environment. The new framework offers persons who wish to conduct these electronic trading systems a choice to register as national securities exchanges or as broker-dealers.[101]

---

101 *See* Regulation of Exchanges and Alternative Trading Systems, Exchange Act Release No. 40,760, 63 Fed. Reg. 70,844, 70,847 (Dec. 22, 1998). *See also* Regulation of Exchanges and Alternative Trading Systems, Exchange Act Release No. 39,884, 63 Fed. Reg. 23,504 (Apr. 29, 1998) (Proposing Release); Regulation of Exchanges, Exchange Act Release No. 38,672, 62 Fed. Reg. 30,485 (June 4, 1997) (Concept Release). For a discussion of Commission regulation of alternative trading systems, *see Comment, Move Over Tickertape, Here Comes the Cyber-Exchange: The Rise of Internet-Based Securities Trading Systems*, 47 CATH. U.L. REV. 1009 (1998) (advocating the creation of a new "national securities association" to operate as a self-regulatory organization for all alternative trading systems).

The alternative trading systems are defined and the choices to the actor are designed to reduce regulatory problems. *See* Regulation of Exchanges and Alternative Trading Systems, 63 Fed. Reg. at 70,846 (noting that the new regulatory framework "is flexible enough to accommodate the evolving technology of, and benefits provided by, alternative trading systems"). New Rule 3a1-1 grants an exemption from regulation as an exchange to alternative trading systems in compliance with new Regulation ATS and meeting other conditions. *See id.* at 70,917, 17 C.F.R. §240.3a1-1(a). New Regulation ATS requires alternative trading systems choosing to register as broker-dealers to comply with enhanced regulation. *See id.* at 70,921-25, 17 C.F.R. §242.300-.303 (Regulation ATS).

Regulation ATS generally defines an "alternative trading system" as an entity "that constitutes . . . a market place or facilities for bringing together purchasers and sellers of securities or for otherwise performing with respect to securities the functions commonly performed by a stock exchange" and does not set rules governing subscribers' conduct (except on the exchange) nor does it discipline them (other than by exclusion). *See id.* at 70,922, 17 C.F.R. §242.300(a). *See also* Regulation of Exchanges, 62 Fed. Reg. at 30,486 n.1

B. Securities Lawmakers' Response to the Internet Environment: Substance, Enforcement, Mechanisms for Change, and Methods of Change

1.   Impact on the Substance of the Securities Laws

Internet trading sites change not only the mode of trading among investors but also the nature and institutional structure of traditional securities markets. Trading sites are fundamentally different from securities exchanges. They are operated by different actors with different incentives and different rewards. Thus, Internet trading sites provide different institutional infrastructures for securities trading. This raises the question of how the new type of market affects the policies underlying securities markets regulation and the rules codifying those policies.

A textual analysis of the definition of "exchange" in the Securities Exchange Act of 1934[102] is not helpful. There are no guides in the existing legislation to interpret the Internet trading "exchanges" as the new trading sites. They were not anticipated by

---

(noting that the term "alternative trading system" is used in the release "to refer generally to automated systems that centralize, display, match, cross, or otherwise execute trading interest, but that are not currently registered with the Commission as national securities exchanges or operated by a registered securities association").

An alternative trading system regulated under Regulation ATS must register as a broker-dealer; file a notice of operation as an alternative trading system; allow Commission examinations, inspections, and investigations; and meet recordkeeping, reporting, and confidentiality requirements. A system with high trading volume must also provide access to publicly displayed orders. A system with 20 percent or more of the trading volume in an equity security (or certain debt securities) must also provide fair access and meet capacity, integrity, and security requirements. *See* Regulation of Exchanges and Alternative Trading Systems, 63 Fed. Reg. at 70,922-24, 17 C.F.R. §242.301(b).

In addition, the Commission adopted Rule 3b-16 to revise the definition of "exchange" to include an entity that "brings together the orders for securities of multiple buyers and sellers" and "uses established, non-discretionary methods (whether by providing a trading facility or by setting rules) under which such orders interact with each other, and the buyers and sellers entering such orders agree to the terms of a trade." *Id.* at 70,918, 17 C.F.R. §240.3b-16(a). *See also id.* at 70,848 (noting that the new definition includes markets engaging in activities functionally equivalent to traditional exchanges). The new definition does not include "bulletin board types of systems" that display "orders" but allow subscribers to contact each other and agree to terms outside the system. *See id.* at 70,850 & n.47 (citing no-action letters involving issuer trading sites).

102 *See* 15 U.S.C. §78c(a)(1).

Congress; they involve not only a new and different technology but also a very different structure and participating actors.

The underlying policies and values of the Act may be affected by the trading sites. The results of their regulation are hard to predict and may lead to new policies and values or to reinforced current policies and values underlying the law. In sum, trading sites can put in question the current fundamental policies of the law and require a different regulatory regime altogether.

2. Impact on Enforcement Mechanisms

Presumably, trading sites do not pose enforcement problems for the Commission. However, they pose serious enforcement problems for investors. As discussed above, investors may need new and other guarantors of the trading contracts among them and some new mechanisms to ensure the performance of the trades regardless of price fluctuations. It is difficult, however, to envision which mechanism would effectively enforce the traders' contracts. Presumably we can create mechanisms for guaranteeing the execution of the trades among individual traders. Such guarantees may be offered by the promoters of the sites or by third parties, and many other possibilities come to mind. We can create a link to a national depository that would confirm trades upon proof of payment. The costs of the new mechanisms must be evaluated as experience about the sites is gathered.

3. The Choice of Adaptive Mechanisms and Method of Adaptation

The first question that trading sites raise is: Which of the mechanisms for change is best suited to determine the adaptation of the securities laws to the new Internet trading sites: Congress, the courts, the Commission, or the markets?

Congress should not legislate new regulation for the trading sites. There is little experience on how these sites function and the consequences of their operations. Congress cannot experiment in allowing piecemeal limited use of the sites nor monitor the problems they raise and the problems they solve.[103]

---

103 The failure of Congress to develop appropriate regulation in the related field of telecommunications law is chronicled in Monroe E. Price & John F. Duffy, *Technological Change and Doctrinal Persistence: Telecommunications Reform in Congress and the Court*, 97 Colum. L. Rev. 976, 977-79 (1997) ("In Congress, we see an institution bold in word, but incremental in deed."). Price and Duffy explain that the Telecommunications Act of 1996 merely "establishes a framework for the next round of conflict—conflict that will take place in courts, regulatory agencies, and the marketplace." *Id.* at 978.

The courts are also not the appropriate mechanism for adapting the securities laws to the trading sites. Courts cannot act unless they are requested to do so in the case of conflict among parties. Besides, courts are not equipped to conduct the study necessary to design a regulatory system nor to enforce such a system. Presumably, if courts were asked to determine whether trading sites are exchanges, they would use the policy analysis adopted in the *VALIC* case[104] and impose the current securities laws on such sites, awaiting the Commission's adaptation of the law to these new "exchanges."

This situation is precisely one that requires experimentation by an administrative agency.[105] First, the values and policies underlying the securities acts support implementation of new technology and trading sites. Second, the Commission has authorized trading sites under certain conditions.[106] These conditions might be strict at the outset and then relaxed as more experience is gathered respecting any problems that these sites pose.[107] Moreover, the Commission has expressed that it is "mindful of the benefits of increasing use of new technologies for investors and the markets, and has encouraged experimentation and innovation by adopting flexible interpretations of the federal securities laws."[108]

---

104 *See SEC v. Variable Annuity Life Ins. Co. of Am.*, 359 U.S. 65, 76 (1959) (Brennan, J., concurring) (examining whether holders of investments need the protection of the securities acts).

105 Professor Lessig suggests a similar approach to the regulation of cyberspace, though he suggests a different method for getting there. He argues that common law should set the boundaries of cyberspace because its "undefined potential" requires "lots of room for democratic experimentation." Lawrence Lessig, *The Path of Cyberlaw*, 104 Yale L.J. 1743, 1753 (1995). "Experimentation, because stable doctrine is only built upon the ground of long-standing experimentation." *Id.*

106 *See, e.g.*, Real Goods Trading Corp., SEC No-Action Letter, (1996-1997 Transfer Binder) Fed. Sec. L. Rep. CCH ¶77,226, *at* 77,131 (June 24, 1996).

107 If we follow the logic of Professor George L. Priest, to the extent that any of these new regulations are inefficient, courts will either overturn them or construe them in a manner which creates a more efficient regime. *See* George L. Priest, *The Common Law Process and the Selection of Efficient Rules*, 6 J. Legal Stud. 65, 73 (1977) ("Where government suits are brought under legal rules that are inefficient, the stakes will be higher and defendants will be more likely to resist the suits and force litigation.").

108 SEC: Report to the Congress: The Impact of Recent Technological Advances on the Securities Markets, *available at* https://www.sec.gov/news/studies/techrp97.htm (last visited Dec. 20, 2023).

If the Commission approached the issue by imposing on trading sites the regulations applicable to exchanges as they exist today, it is likely to freeze the development of trading sites. These sites cannot operate under the current exchange regulation and to change the regulation would require congressional action, which, as we noted above, is not the appropriate adaptive mechanism in this case.

This brings us to the markets. Could the markets be left to adapt and shape market customs to regulate trading sites? Leaving the markets to develop best practices for trading sites is a very attractive suggestion. The hand of the multitudes of investors and the promoters' behavioral adaptive mode of trial and error might offer regulators a proven, optimal model of regulation. If markets also provide effective sanctions to those who violate adapted customs, perhaps no government regulation would be necessary. Further, market "creeping" regulation may avoid unanticipated consequences, which government regulations tend to bring as side effects, regardless of how well-intentioned and how focused regulators try to be.

I reject markets as a sole mechanism for adapting the securities laws to trading sites for a number of reasons. First, nothing concerning trading sites suggests that the fundamental policies of ensuring investor confidence and facilitating capital should be changed. These remain the main guides to the institutional structures of the markets. Inexpensive enforcement of trades must be secured. Prices must be published. Segmentation should be avoided. Yet it is not clear that markets would heed these policies and ensure compliance with them. If markets would have heeded these policies in the past, we would not have government securities regulation today.

Second, the stakes are too high to allow promoters to break, on their own and for their own benefit, new grounds in shaping the new institutions for markets, especially when these new markets are still small. Third, and most importantly, failure to ensure the integrity of the new markets may taint existing markets. Investors do not always make refined distinctions when they are defrauded or find they made decisions without sufficient information. Paradoxically, "free" markets require a regulatory infrastructure.[109]

---

109 *See, e.g.*, Deborah A. Ballam, *The Evolution of the Government-Business Relationship in the United States: Colonial Times to Present*, 31 Am. Bus. L.J. 553 (1994) (describing, among other things, how elements of the business

This infrastructure can be developed by the actors, such as broker-dealers and other intermediaries. However, infrastructure is less likely when markets develop by suppliers of sites and actions of investors. Neither the suppliers nor the investors are likely to have sufficient identity of interest to combine in self-regulatory organizations and provide the infrastructure.[110]

Leaving the markets alone to design the trading sites is not the answer. Leaving the Commission alone to design a regulatory scheme for the trading sites is also not the full answer. It seems that we should develop a close interactive adaptive system between the markets and the Commission. In fact, such an interactive approach is to some extent already being practiced by the Commission. The Commission publishes many company proposals for comments; commissioners and staff meet regularly with industry representatives, lawyers, and consumer representative groups. The industry may make presentations to the staff to educate and provide information. Lawyers seek and receive the staff's interpretation of the law *ex ante*, while offering the staff information about events in the markets. This does not mean that the parties bare their hearts to each other. Neither the staff nor the industry are fully informative, but a substantial amount of information is exchanged between them in a search for a solution satisfactory to both parties.

It seems that the trading sites require a period of experimentation, with controlled limits, under close monitoring of the Commission. It may well be that this method is beginning to take shape in the form of no-action letters that the staff has issued for issuer trading sites. The method of change in this case is therefore complex, slow, experimental, and public. This method is, of course, remindful of the method by which markets adapt their customary law. It may well be that we have reached a stage where law's adaptation requires interaction between markets and agencies. Markets represent an amalgamation of perspectives of different actors driven by differing interests, understandings, and levels of information. In the case of securities markets and other

---

community have supported a strong role for the government in creating the environment in which business operates); Joseph P. Tomain & Sidney A. Shapiro, *Analyzing Government Regulation*, 49 ADMIN. L. REV. 377 (1997) (explaining how governmental regulation attempts to remedy market failures).

110 *See* Tamar Frankel, *Should Funds and Investment Advisers Form a Self-Regulatory Organization?*, *in* THE FINANCIAL SERVICES REVOLUTION 447 (Clifford E. Kirsch ed., 1997).

markets, this amalgamation is translated into the price in dollars. The dollars become the common denominator.

In the case of market custom, however, the amalgamation of perspectives of different actors, driven by various interests and understandings and levels of information, does not always reflect a common denominator. Although custom represents a pattern of behavior that is followed by an increasing number of actors, this pattern is not transparent, nor clearly predictable. When regulatory agencies adopt a custom or "best practices" of an industry, the agencies can meld together the various aspects of the custom-producing actors; in some respect the agencies provide the missing common denominator that money would have provided in the form of price, to create better rules while subsuming the substance of the customs.

How do agencies collate and meld together items that do not emanate from similar sources or for similar reasons (sometimes from conflicting reasons)? Put differently, how do agencies generalize disparate items that are generated by disparate driving forces and for different reasons? The answer is: not by mathematical addition. Rather, a "soft process" of judgment based on information, context, and experience brings about a coherent rule based on the substance of the custom. This process is demonstrated by the restatements of the laws and codification of uniform laws—drafting, articulation of norms, and rationalization of market customs.

One form of interaction between the staff of the Commission and industry is worth noting; this form is not unique to the agency and is practiced, in different ways, by other agencies as well. The Commission's staff has been offering the public informal views on proposed activities that may raise issues under the federal securities laws.[111] These letters offer a number of advantages.

The letters inform the staff about proposed transactions in the market, possible legal barriers to novel transactions, and problems they might pose for investors. The letters help avoid or reduce enforcement by litigation and leave some room for restructuring

---

111 In response to letters of inquiry, the staff issues "no-action letters" stating that the staff will not recommend to the Commission an enforcement action if the proposed activities take place. *See* Monthly Publication of List of Significant Letters Issued by the Division of Corporate Finance, Securities Act Release No. 5691, 41 Fed. Reg. 13,682 (Mar. 31, 1976) (describing the no-action letter process). Hence the name: "no-action letters." For a discussion of the no-action letter process, *see* 1 Tamar Frankel & Arthur B. Laby, THE REGULATION OF MONEY MANAGERS 144-1 to 1-184 (Ann Taylor Schwing, ed. 2023).

and legitimizing proposed activities. No-action letters benefit the public and strengthen the rule of law by publicizing the staff's interpretation and application of the securities laws.[112] The business community has come to depend on the consistent application of the letters' rulings in making business decisions. The process facilitates business transactions, especially novel transactions, that may not exactly fit within the regulatory framework when the interpretation of the law applicable to them is uncertain.

The main source of the staff's authority is its discretion to recommend that the Commission prosecute violations of the statutes under its jurisdiction.[113] The weight given to the staff's letters depends mostly on the type of reasoning on which the decision is based. When the letter represents the opinion of the staff on a particular legal issue,[114] the letter is likely to be viewed as a precedent on the legal issues in the particular fact pattern, at least until it is reversed by the staff, the Commission, or the courts.[115] Courts, however, often defer to the staff's legal interpretation and expertise.[116] When the staff grants a no-action position even "without necessarily agreeing with" the requestor's legal position,[117] such a letter has less weight than an interpretative

---

112 In recent years the staff has resorted to letters to the Investment Company Institute, expressing the staff's concerns about certain issues or events. *See, e.g.*, Investment Co. Inst., 1993 SEC No-Act. Lexis 673 (Apr. 19, 1993). These letters help inform the industry about the staff's concerns, and often elicit the industry's response by voluntary self-enforcement or self-studies that provide information to the staff and can result in self-enforcement. *See* Investment Co. Inst., Report to the Division of Investment Management, U.S. Securities and Exchange Commission, Implementation of the Institute's Recommendations on Personal Investing (1995), *summarized in* Mutual Funds Have Implemented Institute's Recommendations on Personal Investing, ICI Survey Finds, PR Newswire, Apr. 21, 1995, *available in* LEXIS, News Library, Arcnws File.

113 *See* 1 Tamar Frankel & Arthur B. Laby, The Regulation of Money Managers 2-68 (Ann Taylor Schwing, ed. 2023). Therefore, no-action letters state that the staff grants or denies assurance that it will not recommend an enforcement action to the Commission.

114 Usually the request letter analyzes the law and the staff may either agree with the position in the letters of request or with part of the position, or offer its own interpretation, leading to the no-action position. *See id.*

115 *See id.* at 2-68.1 to 2-69.

116 *See id.*

117 The main reason for such letters is that, although the proposed activities are impermissible, or it is unclear whether they are permissible, the staff will not recommend enforcement action, presumably because the Commission's resources would be better employed otherwise. *See id.*

letter.[118] It might still be used by third parties if the facts at hand closely resemble those cited in the letter.[119]

Formally and officially, no-action letters have no value as precedents.[120] Neither the Commission nor the staff are bound by these no-action letters.[121] Yet, practicing attorneys and academics view no-action letters as a source of law, and they are considered precedents by parties other than the recipients, providing a partial safe harbor and guidance to practitioners.[122] The letters augment the limited number of court cases and Commission interpretations and are sometimes the only authoritative interpretations of the Act. Perhaps the paucity of judicial decisions may be attributed in part to no-action letters that meet the needs of the parties and the industry. Moreover, the no-action process is generally less costly than a formal exemptive application or Commission administrative action, and far less costly than litigation.

So long as the staff and the Commission value no-action letters, they will accord them precedential weight. If people could not rely on these letters, people would cease to ask for them, and the benefits from such letters to the staff, the Commission, the industry, and the parties would be lost. That may be the reason why the staff is concerned with uniformity and predictability of no-action letters. The frequency with which the staff reverses prior letters differs depending on changes in the business environment and the industry, the problems that the letters addressed, and the unintended consequences that such letters brought about.[123]

---

118 *See id.*

119 A third type of reasoning is that the proposed activities are very unique and in all probability will not be repeated by the requestor or anyone else. Although in most letters the staff emphasizes that the letters have no precedential value and are limited to the particular case, in these unique cases the language of the emphasis is stronger. *See id.* A favorable response limited to a unique situation is a far weaker precedent for an identical set of facts in a similar context.

120 *See id.* at 2-68.1 to 2-69.

121 *See id.* at 2-68.1 to 2-70.

122 *See id.*; Simon M. Lorne et al., Securities Law Considerations Affecting Employee Benefit Plans A-8 (BNA Corp. Practice Series No. 44-2nd, 1997) ("Persons obtaining no-action letters are entitled to rely on them, but generally other persons are not entitled to so rely. However, since 1971 . . . (the Commission) has at least moved toward allowing a more general reliance although not as a formal policy.").

123 *See* 1 Tamar Frankel & Arthur B. Laby, THE REGULATION OF MONEY MANAGERS 2-68.1 to 2-69 (Ann Taylor Schwing ed. 2023).

Thus, the letters provide substantial comfort to their recipients even in private litigation.[124]

In some respects no-action letters are similar to judicial decisions because they are based on specific fact situations, rely on precedents, and constitute precedents, especially when they provide analysis and reasoning. The letters differ from a judicial decision because they are given with little express legal authority and are granted *ex ante*, and not *ex post*, as a result of conflict. The letters are similar to customary law. Their age and extent of following adds to their precedential weight. Their flexibility allows for adjusting law to changing circumstances. For law's adaptation to the Internet environment, they may be a most appropriate tool.

CONCLUSION

This article offers a first step towards an examination of adaptation of law to a changing environment of the actors that are regulated by law. I suggest a model of law as a structured, adaptive, self-replicating system of coercive communications regulating relationships among types of actors (individuals or groups). The three-part structure of the law consists of substantive communications that differ in their degree of generality (specific cases, rules, policies, and values), mechanisms for enforcing the law, and mechanisms for adapting law when the actors that are regulated experience a new environment (legislatures, administrative agencies, courts, the markets), using methods of adaptation (textual analysis, analogy, and policy analysis).

When the environment of regulated actors changes rapidly, as it changes today and is likely to change in the future, a new combined mechanism of markets and agencies is being developed to adapt the law accordingly. This new mechanism and its methods of adaptation invite a close examination and empirical study, for I believe this is the future mechanism for legal change.

---

124 *See id.* at 2-68.1 to 2-70. In some cases courts may refuse to defer to the staff's interpretation of the law; for example, if the issue does not involve a matter within the special expertise of the staff or when the Commission is the plaintiff—to avoid a result that the agency would be both prosecutor and legislator. *See id.* at 2-68.1 to 2-70. *See also New York City Employees' Retirement Sys. v. American Brands, Inc.*, 634 F. Supp. 1382, 1389 n.6 (S.D.N.Y. 1986) (refusing to defer where issue does not involve matter within special expertise of staff); *SEC v. Energy Group, Inc.*, 459 F. Supp. 1234, 1238 (S.D.N.Y. 1978) (refusing to defer where Commission is plaintiff).

Appendix

Books

_____, Domain Name Handbook, International Forum on the White Paper (IFWP)

_____, FIFRA Rule 2210

_____, National Association of Securities Dealers, NASD Manual

_____, Special Forum on Trust in and Between Organizations, 23 Academy of Mgmt. Rev. 459 (Sim B. Sitkin et al. eds., 1998)

_____, Symposium, The Internet and Small Business Capital Formation, 2 J. Small & Emerging Bus. L. (1998)

Austin, John, The Province of Jurisprudence Determined and the Uses of the Study of Jurisprudence (1954)

Axelrod, Robert, The Complexity of Cooperation: Agent-Based Models of Competition and Cooperation (1997)

Barber, Bernard, The Logic and Limits of Trust (1983)

Baumol, William J., et al., Contestable Markets and The Theory of Industry Structure (1982)

Bok, Sissela, A Strategy for Peace (1989)

Calamari, John D. & Joseph M. Perillo, The Law of Contracts (4th ed. 1998)

Chisum, Donald S., et al., Principles of Patent Law (2d ed. 2001)

Cooter, Robert & Thomas Ulen, Law and Economics (2000)

Davis, Morton D., Game Theory: A Nontechnical Introduction (2003)

Drexler, K. Eric, Engines of Creation (1986)

Farnsworth, E. Allan, Farnsworth on Contracts (4th ed. 2019), updated by Zachary Wolfe

Frankel, Tamar, Securitization: Structured Financing, Financial Assets Pools, and Asset-Backed Securities (2d ed., Ann Taylor Schwing, ed. 2005)

Frankel, Tamar & Arthur B. Laby, The Regulation of Money Managers (Ann Taylor Schwing, 3d ed. 2023)

Fukuyama, Francis, Great Disruption: Human Nature and the Reconstitution of Social Order (1999)

Fukuyama, Francis, Trust: The Social Virtues and the Creation of Prosperity (1995)

Gambetia, Diego, The Sicilian Mafia: The Business of Private Protection (1993)

Govier, Trudy, Social Trust and Human Communities (1997)

Granit, Ragnar, The Purposive Brain (1980)

Holmes, John G. & John K. Rempel, Close Relationships (Clyde Hendrick ed. 1989)

Keeton, W. Page et al., Prosser and Keeton on the Law of Torts 33 (W. Page Keeton ed., 5th ed. 1984)

Kramer, Roderick M. and Tom R. Tyler, Trust in Organizations, Frontiers of Theory and Research (1996)

Lessig, Lawrence, Code and Other Laws of Cyberspace (1999)

Luhmann, Niklas, Trust and Power (1980)

Posner, Richard A., Economic Analysis of Law (5th ed. 1998)

Postel, Jon, Domain Name System Structure and Delegation (1994)

Solomon, Lewis D., et al., Corporations: Law and Policies: Materials and Problems (1982)

Spar, Debora L., Ruling the Waves (2003)

Tye, William B., The Theory of Contestable Markets (1990)

Whitney, John O., The Economics of Trust: Liberating Profits and Restoring Corporate Vitality (1996)

Williams, J.D., The Compleat Strategist (rev. ed. 1966)

Ziegler, Rolf, Trust and the Reliability of Expectations, Rationality and Society (1998)

Articles

Alvey, Jennifer L., Government Group Advising ICANN Wants Nations to Control Country Code Domains, Electronic Com. & L. Rep. (BNA), Mar. 8, 2000

Alvey, Jennifer L., Internet May Have New .com-Type Domains Soon if Net Authority Acts on Schedule, Electronic Com. & L. Rep. (BNA), Mar. 15, 2000

Ballam, Deborah A., The Evolution of the Government-Business Relationship in the United States: Colonial Times to Present, 31 Am. Bus. L.J. 553 (1994)

Baxter, Hugh, Autopoiesis and the "Relative Autonomy" of Law, 19 Cardozo L. Rev. 1987 (1998)

Bernstein, Lisa, Merchant Law in a Merchant Court: Rethinking the Code's Search for Immanent Business Norms, 144 U. Pa. L. Rev. 1765 (1996)

Bhattacharya, Rajeev et al., A Formal Model of Trust Based on Outcomes *in* The Academy of Mgmt. Rev., Special Forum on Trust in and Between Organizations (Sim B. Sitkin et al. eds., 1998)

Black, Bernard S., & Ronald J. Gilson, Venture Capital and The Structure of Capital Markets: Banks versus Stock Markets, 47 J. Fin. Econ. 243 (1998)

Booth, Richard A., The Uncertain Case for Regulating Program Trading, 1994 Colum. Bus. L. Rev. 1

Budnitz, Mark E., Stored Value Cards and the Consumer: The Need for Regulation, 46 Am. U.L. Rev. 1027 (1997)

Cella III, Joseph F., & John Reed Stark, SEC Enforcement and the Internet: Meeting the Challenge of the Next Millenium, A Program for the Eagle and the Internet, 52 Bus. Law. 815 (1997)

Chapman, Bruce, Trust, Economic Rationality, and the Corporate Fiduciary Obligation, 43 U. Toronto L.J. 547 (1993)

Choi, Stephen J., Gatekeepers and the Internet: Rethinking the Regulations of Small Business Capital Formation, 2 J. Small & Emerging Bus. L. 27 (1998)

Colman, Andrew M., Game Theory and Its Applications: In the Social and Biological Sciences (2d ed. 1999)

Duncan, Beth, Wallman Suggests SEC Should Be Open to Seminal, Not Incremental, Change, 29 Sec. Reg. & L. Rep. (BNA) 993 (July 18, 1997)

Frankel, Tamar, Fiduciary Law, 71 Cal. L. Rev. 795 (1983)

Frankel, Tamar, The Legal Infrastructure of Markets: The Role of Contract and Property Law, 73 B.U.L. Rev. 389 (1993)

Frankel, Tamar, Should Funds and Investment Advisers Establish a Self-regulatory Organization?, in The Financial Services Revolution, Understanding the Changing Roles of Banks, Mutual Funds and Insurance Companies, (Clifford E. Kirsch ed., 1997)

Frankel, Tamar, The Internet, Securities Regulation, and Theory of Law, 73 Chi.-Kent. L. Rev. 1319 (1998)

Frankel, Tamar, Trusting and Non-Trusting on the Internet, 81 B.U.L. Rev. 457 (2001)

Frankel, Tamar, The Managing Lawmaker in Cyberspace: A Power Model, 27 Brook. J. Int'l L. 859 (2002)

Frankel, Tamar, Governing by Negotiation: The Internet Naming System, 12 Cardozo J. Int'l & Comp. L. 449 (2004)

Froomkin, A. Michael, Reinventing the Government Corporation, 1995 U. Ill. L. Rev. 543 (1995)

Froomkin, A. Michael, Wrong Turn in Cyberspace: Using ICANN to Route Around the APA and the Constitution, 50 Duke L.J. 17 (2000)

Geist Michael A., Goverments and Country-Code Top Level Domains: A Global Survey

Geist, Michael A., The Reality of Bytes: Regulating Economic Activity in the Age of the Internet, 73 Wash. L. Rev. 521 (1998)

Hardin, Russell, Trust and Trustworthiness, 81 B.U.L. Rev. 495 (2001)

Johnson, David & David Post, And How Shall the Net Be Governed?: A Meditation on the Relative Virtues of Decentralized, Emergent Law, in Coordinating the Internet (Brian Kahin & James H. Keller eds., 1997)

Johnson, David R., & David Post, Law and Borders—The Rise of Law in Cyberspace, 48 Stan. L. Rev. 1367 (1996)

Kostritsky, Juliet P., Bargaining With Uncertainty, Moral Hazard, and Sunk Costs: A Default Rule For Precontractual Negotiations, 44 Hastings L.J. 621 (1993)

Langevoort, Donald C., Information Technology and the Structure of Securities Regulation, 98 Harv. L. Rev. 747 (1985)

Lessig, Lawrence, Preface to Trust, 81 B.U.L. Rev. 329 (2001)

Lessig, Lawrence, The Path of Cyberlaw, 104 Yale L.J. 1743 (1995)

Lessig, Lawrence, The Zones of Cyberspace, 48 Stan. L. Rev. 1403 (1996)

McDonald, Bruce A., International Intellectual Property Rights, 35 Int'l Law 465 (2001)

McKenzie, Diana J.P., Commerce on the Net: Surfing Through Cyberspace Without Getting Wet, 14 J. Marshall J. Computer & Info. L. 247 (1996)

Mitchell, Lawrence E., Fairness and Trust in Corporate Law, 43 Duke L.J. 425 (1993)

Mooney, Jr., Charles W., Property, Credit, and Regulation Meet Information Technology: Clearance and Settlement in the Securities Markets, 55 Law & Contemp. Probs. 131 (1992)

Nissenbaum, Helen, Securing Trust Online: Wisdom or Oxymoron? 81 B.U.L. Rev. 101 (2001)

Popper, Karl R., The Rationality of Scientific Revolutions: Selection Versus Instruction, *in* The Myth of the Framework (M.A. Notturno ed., 1994)

Potter, Mary C., Remembering, 3 Thinking: An Invitation to Cognitive Science (Daniel N. Osherson & Edward E. Smith eds., 1990)

Price, Monroe E., & John F. Duffy, Technological Change and Doctrinal Persistence: Telecommunications Reform in Congress and the Court, 97 Colum. L. Rev. 976 (1997)

Priest, George L., The Common Law Process and the Selection of Efficient Rules, 6 J. Legal Stud. 65 (1977)

Rastogi, Dipak K., Living Without Borders *in* Understanding Business Environments (2000)

Rotter, J. B., 35 Interpersonal Trust, Trustworthiness, and Gullibility, Am. Psych., (1980)

Sableman, Mark, ICANN Faces Major Challenge with Country Codes, Nat'l L.J., Dec. 18, 2000

Smith, Brian W., & Ramsey J. Wilson, How Best to Guide the Evolution of Electronic Currency Law, 46 Am. U.L. Rev. 1105 (1997)

Spangnolo, Giancarlo, Social Relationships and Cooperation in Organizations, 38 J. Economic Behavior & Organization 1 (1999)

Tomain, Joseph P., & Sidney A. Shapiro, Analyzing Government Regulation, 49 Admin. L. Rev. 377 (1997)

Von Arx, Kim G. & Gregory R. Hagen, Sovereign Domains, A Declaration of Independence of ccTLDs from Foreign Control, 9 Rich. J.L. & Tech. 4 (2002)

Wallman, Steven M.H., Regulating in a World of Technological and Global Change, Metropolitan Corp. Couns. (Oct. 1996)

Zak, Ann Marie, et al., Assessments of Trust in Intimate Relationships and Self-Perception Process, 138(2) J. Soc. Psych. 217 (1998)

Comment, Move Over Tickertape, Here Comes the Cyber-Exchange: The Rise of Internet-Based Securities Trading Systems, 47 Cath. U.L. Rev. 1009 (1998)

Comment, Who Needs Wall Street? The Dilemma of Regulating Securities Trading in Cyberspace, 5 CommLaw Conspectus 305 (1997)

Note, The Application of Securities Laws in Cyberspace: Jurisdictional and Regulatory Problems Posed by Internet Securities Transactions, 18 Hastings Comm. & Ent. L.J. 901 (1996)